A SENSE OF HOME

Helen James is a leading Irish designer – best known for her Considered range at Dunnes Stores – and her much-loved food blogging. She previously worked as Design Director for Donna Karan Home in New York and was co-presenter of RTÉ's Home of the Year. She is a mother to three boys and lives in Dublin. *A Sense of Home* is her first book.

A SENSE OF HOME

EAT | MAKE | SLEEP | LIVE

HELEN JAMES

First published in 2017 by Hachette Books Ireland
An Hachette UK Company

1

A CIP catalogue record for this title is available from the British Library.

ISBN: 978 1 473 63390 2

Typeset in Baskerville by Anú Design, Tara
Book text design by Anú Design, Tara
Cover design by cabinlondon.co.uk
Printed and bound in Germany by Mohn Media GmbH

Hachette Books Ireland policy is to use papers that are natural, renewable and recyclable products and made from wood grown in sustainable forests. The logging and manufacturing processes are expected to conform to the environmental regulations of the country of origin.

Hachette Books Ireland
8 Castlecourt Centre
Castleknock
Dublin 15
Ireland

A division of Hachette UK,
Carmelite House, 50 Victoria Embankment, London EC4Y 0DZ, England
www.hachettebooksireland.ie

Contents

To my mum and dad –

two of the most interesting people I've ever met

Exploring
Your Senses,
and Mine

A house is a building ...

A home is a living thing

CREATING A HOME, a personal haven, is not just about painting a wall and putting down a rug. Now more than ever, we want our homes to be a true reflection of ourselves. Your home is so much greater than a house, more than four walls and a roof. It is a combination of your senses, of the familiar, the loved, the traditional. It's the warm feeling of coming through your door at the end of a long day, or indeed after time spent away. "It is so good to be home," your nervous system relates, as it lets go and unwinds.

Homes should nurture and nourish us, be a private sanctuary, a deeply personal place where friends and family gather and celebrate.

Every time you walk into someone's home, including your own, you are experiencing it with all of your senses, even though you may not be consciously aware of it …

The feel of a floor underfoot, hard wood, soft pile carpet? Tiles?

The smell of a burning fire or a delicious meal cooking.

The sound of music, a familiar voice, or just as important, the lack of sound – peace and sanctuary.

The taste of your favourite food, memories of childhood flavours.

The colours and the combination of colour.

You are experiencing all of your surroundings with all of these senses and they are making you feel at ease or on edge, comfortable or anxious, sometimes in subtle ways that you may not even realise.

So, how can you become more aware of these things and then fine-tune them to meet your own exact preferences? The first step is to become aware of them, and then to apply what you have learned to your surroundings.

What should your bedroom *feel* like? What should your living room *smell* like? We should approach the creation and shaping of our home with all of these senses as our guide. How can you make each room – even the smallest room – into a place that gives you the best and most personal experience of it possible?

I want to show you how you can tune in to your surroundings and create a home that not only looks good but smells good, where the air is as clean as possible, where beautiful textures and surfaces abound and where you can take the time you need to feed your soul! By exploring what you like and applying this to your home you can create a deeply individual space where you can entertain, luxuriate in food you have prepared and treat yourself with indulgent natural bodycare products that will nourish your body and soul.

{ Every room should have a plant, a book and at least one natural object. }

They say only 10 per cent of communication is through speech; well, I feel the same way about how our homes look. So much emphasis is placed on how we see a room, but have you ever walked into a room that *smelled* really bad? In that moment, nothing else mattered, right? Who cares what colour the walls are or how many cushions are on the sofa – if there is a bad smell it is hard to focus on anything else: equally, a pleasing smell can help relax you and make you appreciate your surroundings more. When the air is clean and full of oxygen it helps us to rejuvenate and regenerate; equally, stale air, that could be harbouring toxins, can drag us down and make us lethargic.

All of our senses are sending messages to our brain every moment of the day but most of the time we are not aware of them. If you start paying attention to your senses and tuning in to them, it can help you create a truly individual home that will nourish and nurture you.

Today, in a digital world where screens take up so much of our time, many of us have become cut off from fully experiencing our senses – this is why it's more important than ever to pay attention to them.

Small changes can have a big impact on the way you experience your environment. This is not about big, expensive renovations or remodelling, but about subtle things you can do to your home and for yourself to make being at home an experience that you relish, that supports and nurtures you. It is about enjoying the humanity of your home and what you eat, breathe, apply and put into your body there.

What is the layer that differentiates a home from a house and what differentiates your home from someone else's? The answer of course is *you*. It takes time to know what your style is and how to apply it to your home environment.

Start simply by learning to really connect with things you love, to allow yourself to discover them anew. Filling your home with colours, textures and scents that appeal to you will make your home work for you and ultimately help to make you happy there.

So what do you do to begin creating the home you desire? It's important to think of your house as a whole, rather than a set of rooms. I have a mantra that every room should have *at least* one thing that is handmade or organic in it, a stone, a plant, a handmade bowl, a piece of driftwood. These things connect us with our humanity. So let's begin discovering what the mantra for *your* home will be.

Approaching The Design of your House

How your home looks is probably the thing that people pay most attention to when they are creating it. Of course, I am obsessed with Pinterest and Instagram, I devour magazines (storage issue!) and books on design, but I want to take you beyond pictures, beyond the two-dimensional version of looking for inspiration and beyond looking at what someone else has already done. There is no satisfaction in trying to replicate something from a magazine and often the results can be a disappointment. Let's explore what really speaks to you, ignites your passion and joy and makes you feel comforted and sustained.

Here is a little exercise to get you started.

Think about a picture of a beautiful flower.

Now think about holding that flower in your hand. The two experiences are entirely different. A picture can excite your eyes, but holding the actual flower offers a range of experiences. Is the stem thorny? Are the petals soft? What does it smell like? This is something that you experience in many layers. This is the way I want you to think when creating your home, not just what it looks like but what it feels like, smells like and how you can create the most personal and enticing haven.

Yes of course the picture is still beautiful but holding the flower awakened so many more of your senses. Let's apply that same principle to your home.

When I am designing, whether it is an apron or a mug, nothing beats holding an object in my hand. This is incredibly important for the feel of something, because of course that is something a picture cannot give you, the sense of touch. It awakens our instincts in a way no picture can.

Hold an object in your hand in a colour you love – a pebble, a napkin – place it beside an object of another colour, a feather or an old envelope. Anything that speaks to you in colour, form or feel. This is going to give you something so much more personal and instinctual than simply picking pictures of things that other people have done. Gather paint swatches by all means, but also look to nature for beautiful colours and combinations. You want to train your eye – by continually looking at things and colours you find inspiring you will learn more and more about your taste and what excites you.

Look at a pebble. What colour is it? Grey? What other colours can you see? Are there flecks of black, white? Is it a blue-grey or a red-grey?

The aim is to challenge your preconceptions and open your mind to the subtleties of colour and colour combinations.

Creating a Master Collection

I want you to create a collection of things that speak to you. This is about getting to know your aesthetic self. This may be something you feel like you already have a handle on, or you may feel like you have no idea what your personal interior 'style' is. This exercise will help you, and I hope, train you to look at things in a new way.

You are going to bring together items that speak to your soul.

Begin gathering objects that you connect with, it can be a colour you like, a texture, something scented. Connect with all of your senses: touch, sight, sound, taste, smell.

At this point don't edit or think about it too much. Get a box or basket and fill it with anything that you love or that resonates with you on some level. Walk through every room in your home and select favourite items. They can be anything – a scarf, a small vase, a found pebble, a handwritten note, sweet wrappers, beautiful packaging you have kept, a length of string, a shell.

beeswax
scent

downstairs loo
wall cover

kitchen counter tops

bedroom
wall colour

skirting
bedroom
upstairs
bathroom
wall colour

wood finish
possible
kitchen or
living room
furniture

carpet

downstairs
loo accent

living room
wall colour

kitchen
accent
colour

lemon
scented
soap

living room
textiles

drawer
pulls
& knobs

kitchen
counter
tops
option 2

kitchen cabinets
colour and finish

bathroom tiles

pop of colour
for living room

Don't worry about creating a story, just put them all in one place. When you have built up around 20 items lay them on a table. Now edit. Does everything deserve a place? This collection should really be the essence of what you love. This is no place for the mediocre or indifferent.

Look at each item and ask yourself if you really love it and what is it that you love – is it the colour? Texture? Feel? Shape?

What does the collection say to you? Is there a theme? Is there pattern/lack of pattern? What about texture? Review and analyse your collection. Can you see connections?

Surprises? Are there particular colours that keep popping up? Are there contradictions? These are good!

Look at the objects individually and as a collection. Scribble down whatever comes to mind. Your list might read something like this:

- Natural
- Pink
- Earth
- Wood
- Smooth
- Organic
- Pop

Name your style if you can: urban naturist ... modern organic ... whatever comes to mind. This exercise can really help to identify your own style to yourself and help you avoid mistakes if you are out shopping for pieces for your home.

When you have created and named your items it will give you a clear idea of where you want to go.

Consider this your master collection. It should give you joy when you look at it. Take a photograph of it and keep it on your phone or print it out and place it somewhere where you can see it every day.

You are exploring your creative self, paying attention to your aesthetic.

Now on a piece of paper, or on your computer screen, create headings for every room in your house and list all the things you would like each room to be.

Your bedroom might inspire words like: serene, calm, romance …

Your living room may be comforting, inviting, cosy …

Your kitchen may be functional, earthy, clean …

Now do a quick recce on all the rooms in your house and take a photo of each one as it currently looks. We can often see things in a photograph we don't notice when just looking with the eye. As you continue on your list, also note the aspect and amount of natural light each room gets. North-facing rooms tend to get indirect, cool light, an easterly room will get morning sun and be darker in the evenings, south-facing rooms will get the brightest and warmest light and a westerly room will be darker in the morning and get lovely evening light. This is useful knowledge to have as you are planning your palette, or personal colour scheme, as the light will affect your colours.

Take a look at your list and photographs. Are you close to where you want to be? Which rooms are the furthest away from your ideal and need the most work?

What are the problems and what is working for you?

Write down any major issues and also things that are positive.

For example: Bedroom cluttered, drab, but has lovely evening light.

Living room might be: Lack of storage (toys), comfortable sofa, bad lighting.

When you assess your notes and photos can you move any furniture around to immediately address any of the issues? Can some items be stripped, repainted or repurposed? For example, can a bookshelf move from a living room to a bedroom, or a cabinet from the dining room to the kitchen? Really consider what you have before you venture into shopping or replacing.

This is not about a major renovation, but about making your home your own individual sanctuary that is a true reflection of who you are, and where you have been, and to help you to make it a refuge from the stressful and busy lives we all lead these days.

Make a plan for each room using your master collection as the point of inspiration.

Colour

For many people, including myself, colour is often the starting point for design. Almost everything I design starts somehow with the colour. The palette is the first thing I work on at the beginning of a season. Once it is decided, everything else follows. This can also be true for your home. I could bore you with colour theory and philosophy, but what is much more exciting is your *personal* reaction to colour. Try to be aware of colours you are drawn to. Do you have a favourite skirt, scarf, chair, painting? Think about colours that have appealed to you in your life: a familiar room, a favourite restaurant, a childhood memory. Are there colours that have perhaps become recurring themes in your life, ones that you are constantly drawn to? Wouldn't it be nice to incorporate these into your home? Have you included these colours in your master collection?

Look at ways your master collection can inspire you – are there interesting colour combinations? A trim on a box, a font? All of these can be used to inform your home.

Creating and Using a Personal Palette

You can make a palette now. This is an easy tool to refer to when tackling any room in your house. From one palette there are multiple possibilities, depending on the weight and amount of coverage you give to different colours. If you have one master palette that you constantly refer back to, it means your house will work together as a cohesive whole. Every room should reference the rest of the house.

This can easily be done using colour and also materials. Repeating materials and colours throughout your home helps it to feel harmonious.

If you match your palette to paint swatches now it will make decisions so much easier when you are caught up in the middle of your project. Do remember, though, to test colours in an environment first, as it can change so much depending on the way light falls in a given room throughout the day. And to be open to change – once a wall is painted you may change your mind on an accent colour, opting to go bolder or calm things down. Remember, one of the easiest and most dramatic things you can do to a room is paint it.

To make your palette, buy some samples of the colours that you've identified from your reflections and instincts. Now paint each colour on to a small piece of white card – index cards or blank white postcards would work well, otherwise just make your own by folding a piece of A4 heavy paper or light card in half vertically and horizontally and cut it, giving you 4 x approximately 10 x 15cm pieces of card. Make sure you give dark colours a double coat to get a true version of the colour. Now sort your colours into possible combinations for each room.

Can you push yourself to take a risk? Think of the natural light in the room, the size and amount of wall coverage, the architectural details, or lack of them. You don't need to follow any rules, just keep this in mind when playing with the palettes. Repeating colours from one room to another can help your home to feel like one fluid environment. When you have decided on your palette you should see what those colours actually look like in the rooms. I recommend the decorators' trick of painting a colour onto a large piece of white card at least A3 size (29.7 x 42cm) and

A SENSE OF HOME

Main and secondary colours for (l-r) Bathroom, Kitchen and Bedroom

not directly onto your walls. Now you can move the card around to see what it looks like on different walls. It will change, depending on available light sources, and because it's on the card it will not react with the existing colour on your wall. You can also handily bring a small piece of it with you when shopping for fabrics and accessories. Remember also to sample the trim colour (if it is different from the wall colour) and see how the two

{ One of the easiest and most dramatic things you can do to a room is paint it. }

work together in the room. Paint the trim onto a long piece of card to echo the proportion of the trim-to-wall ratio. Remember that the colour will be more intense when it is painted on all the walls.

For each room, you want to think of the following points:

1. What will the **main** colour be? This is the tone on the largest areas: walls, ceiling and floors.
2. What will the **secondary** colour be? This refers to large items of furniture, it should work with your main colour but not be the same, otherwise you risk boredom.

3. What will **accent** colours be? These are colours for lamps, cushions, vases, etc. You can be most adventurous here; think about contrasts and highlights. It can be useful to leave this colour choice until your room is finished, then you can play around with the accents, making your room more harmonious by choosing tonal colours or more dynamic by going for contrast.

Your colours will most likely cross over a bit between the three areas, but these are general guidelines to get you started.

Don't worry if you're not confident using the boldest colours on your walls – use them instead on accents, in textiles, lighting and in unexpected places like the inside of cupboards (a trick that could make you happy every time you open your wardrobe). Try painting the trim in a contrasting or much deeper hue to add drama to a room.

Small spaces that are not on permanent display at home are a great place to go a bit wild. The downstairs loo is a good example of a place where you can be a bit adventurous and playful. Try a very bright colour, outrageous wallpaper or go rich and dark to create a cocoon-like space. Being bold in a small area first can give you the confidence to take risks in the larger rooms later.

Once you've picked the colour for the walls and trim, what about the rest of the room? I'm all for pushing boundaries with colour but I understand that sometimes people want to be more cautious with big-ticket items. If you are spending a lot of money on a sofa you do not want to make a mistake, and having a new cover made can be almost the same price as a new sofa. On the other hand, a grey sofa in a grey room with a grey carpet, even if you have varying shades, is going to read as very bland. My advice is to try and expand yourself in at least one of these areas – if your walls are painted grey then look back at your palette, is there another colour you can pick for the sofa, a soft terracotta, a navy? Or a pattern – you can keep it dusty and muted if you are feeling timid!

Inspiration from Nature

When working on a personal palette, another source of inspiration I am constantly drawn to is nature. Imagine the colour of lichen on a stick, moss on a stone, flowers and foliage, the feathers on a starling, each stunning in their own way. Take a look at the natural world, and explore a little deeper. Pick up a flower. What colour are the petals? If you look closely you will see there are more colours than may be immediately apparent. Look into the centre of the flower, at the stamen, the stem and the leaves. Take a photo or jot down the colours you see, then think about this the next time you need inspiration in a room.

The texture of lichen growing on a stick could translate into cushions on a sofa or a rug on the floor.

• • • • •

A Story about Wabi-sabi

Many years ago, in the Westmeath village where I lived, there was an old vacant cottage. I paid it no regard other than in many ways it reminded me of my own home, if it had fallen on bad times. Then one day while walking through the village, I noticed that the front door was open. I enquired in the newsagent's next door, knowing of course that the lady behind the counter would be up to date on the news of her neighbour.

She told me it was to be gutted and turned into a doctor's office, and agreed to give me the owner's number.

I returned to my house and immediately rang it with some trepidation. The owner might not like the idea that I had been snooping inside the building, for safety reasons if not for trespassing.

I introduced myself and tentatively explained how I had seen the door open and that there was an old Belfast sink on the floor and if he didn't want it I would love it and would be willing to pay him for it. "Ah sure take it," he said. "Take it and anything else in there that you would like." I thanked him kindly and with enormous gratitude went back to the house in my car and loaded a little table and the Belfast sink into the boot. I then ventured up the stairs where I found a single cast-iron bed and another larger table with a drawer. I also found many old iron hooks lying on the floor. I piled it all into my car. I treated the wood vigorously for woodworm because much as I liked the way it looked, I did not like the idea of welcoming them into my home.

When the fumigation was finished I lifted the little table into my kitchen and placed it in front of the back window. I can clearly remember sitting and looking adoringly at that table as one may gaze on a lover. Is it normal to love a little table this much, I wondered. What I did not know then was that there is a word for this thing that I was feeling: *wabi-sabi*. This is a Japanese phrase for the appreciation of items that are worn and weathered, items with humility, purity and restraint. Its roots lie in Zen Buddhism. It expresses the celebration of the cracked, frayed, aged and authentic. The beauty in the imperfection of nature. It is finding the joy in a lichen-covered stick, a stone, a weathered piece of wood, smooth pebble, a shell.

I think I've embraced the wabi-sabi aesthetic since childhood, when I began collecting natural objects. My grandmother was not happy when she found, under my bed, a vast curated collection of autumn leaves, each one carefully placed on a square tissue from her tissue box. They were, to her eyes, rubbish and litter, but to me they were beautiful treasures – each one individual and beaming with colour and wonder. Later, my friend's father had to plead with me on a tour of Ireland at the age of 12 to please not collect any more stones as the weight of them was dragging the car down.

Wabi simply means humble, tranquil, content. *Sabi* means tarnish, the wear of time, faded. A sabi thing is graceful and dignified and must be earned through time.

{ A true wabi-sabi home should be minimal and free from clutter. }

So the two words together have evolved to mean a humble worn thing with dignity and grace.

A true wabi-sabi home should be minimal and free from clutter. Although I admire the concept, I do not live like this – my instinctual collector tendencies, the reality of life, and motherhood mean it is not for now. But I do apply many principles of wabi-sabi into my home and life and am conscious of keeping a 'wabi mind':

- Items must be beautiful and/or functional
- There is much beauty in the weathered
- There is infinite beauty in nature
- Live in the moment
- Strip away the unnecessary … and then strip it away again.

Getting Light Right

Lighting is something that people often leave as an afterthought, thinking of it as simply functional. The truth is that lighting is of primary importance because it directly affects our mood and demeanour and instantly changes the ambience of a room.

I was at a party recently in a large venue. The music was great, the people were fun, the room was packed, but the lighting was all wrong. It was way too bright. People stood around in huddles anxiously looking over their shoulders, save for one or two brave souls who gave it their all, as others looked on: some jealously, some sniggering-ly. There was just no atmosphere. What was wrong? The lighting. Note: people like dancing in the dark!

So that is only a small example of how the wrong lighting can affect your behaviour and sense of enjoyment. Just think of candlelight, softly glowing table lamps, diffused pools of light and shade. The right lighting helps us to relax and unwind.

The first and most important kind of lighting is the natural light that your house gets. Natural light should be maximised as it has a positive effect on our mood and always provides the most beautiful light, but sometimes it needs a little help. You should already have taken note of the aspect of each room, that is, in which direction it faces. Make sure curtains pull all the way back from windows, not blocking any of the light.

Your home will need three kinds of lighting:
* **Ambient** – the background lighting of overheads and downlights
* **Task** – for doing things like reading and cooking
* **Accent** – the lighting that is there for decoration and drama.

Think about what job lighting needs to do in each room. Kitchens need good lighting for the task of preparing food and being able to see properly while using sharp implements. Bedrooms need reading lights beside the bed and an overhead so you can accurately check your outfit and make-up before

leaving the house. A living room needs lights for reading too, and possibly an overhead. All overheads should be on a dimmer switch, whatever the room. Dimmer switches are a wonderful tool and give you great control over the mood of your room with a very simple turn of a knob. When you've covered these basics, you can then think about areas where you can add drama and atmosphere by playing with the lighting.

Think of those Moroccan metal lampshades with holes punched in them that cast dramatic shadows around the room. Or tall floor lamps that create a warm pool of light in a dark corner of a living room. Fairy lights draped over a mantelpiece or around a mirror that add a pretty, playful vibe. Used correctly, lighting can make your room seem bigger and certainly more interesting. Used incorrectly, it can make you feel uncomfortable and agitated.

Awakening a Sense of Scent

Scent is another powerful tool. It is one of the most evocative stimulators of memories that I know. Years ago I was at a Christmas fair. I began chatting to a lady who had a somewhat random selection of fragrance samples, and she invited me to smell any and all of them. I did. Some were interesting, some were less so and then, suddenly, I raised a tiny bottle to my nose and

had the most overwhelming feeling of comfort, love and soothing calm. It was a little black bottle, a bit dated-looking. "Oh my goodness what is *that*?!" I asked. It was a sample of a perfume that had been around for years and she happened to still have some of it. I asked her if I could keep it and she obliged. I spent the rest of the afternoon sniffing the top of this bottle and each time I had the same reaction, a swirling in the core of my belly and an overwhelming feeling of comfort and calm. Some hours later my mother arrived at the fair, and she saw the tiny bottle in my hand. "Where did you get that?" she enquired. "I haven't seen a bottle of that in years, that was my perfume when you were a little girl …" So even though my conscious mind could not place the scent, somewhere deep inside me it had been filed and kept to remind me of my mother.

This powerful sense is one that is often overlooked when we come to designing our homes. We don't really pay attention to it unless it is quite extreme, but think about your sense of smell for a moment. Retailers are well aware how powerful smell is. Why do you think the fresh smell of baking bread now wafts through most large supermarkets, and the scented candle and perfume businesses are multi-billion-euro industries? But it is not something many of us pay much attention to, save when we buy a perfume or a candle. It would be true to say that each of us has a scent personality, certain scents we are drawn to, be they sweet, woody, fresh or floral.

Do you have a favourite perfume? A favourite flower scent? Most of us are aware of smells we like and don't like. Let's think beyond throwing a few scented candles into a room and instead ponder how smells can have an effect on your mood. Scent is a huge memory trigger that can calm or excite us. Inhaling essential oils triggers the area of the brain which sends messages to other parts of the body, so you can send signals to be alert, serene or calm, depending on what you are doing at that time. The more you know about this, the more control you have over it.

You can become more in tune with your sense of smell and train it. Just as you exercise your muscles to become stronger, so you can train and strengthen your sense of smell by doing some simple exercises.

First list some of your favourite smells. Keep a notebook in your bag and jot down smells that catch your attention. Be alert to them throughout your day. What can you smell when you walk into a coffee shop, for instance? Freshly ground coffee, warm milk, perhaps some pastries baking, some vanilla or chocolate. Note the different scents and write them down in your journal.

Now smell your favourite perfume. Try to decipher it. Can you identify different layers in the scent? Specific notes? In 1916 German psychologist Hans Henning developed the 'odour prism', classifying smells as flowery, fruity, spicy, resinous, burnt and putrid. Thus he tried to identify six scents much like our five senses of taste which are described as sweet, salty, sour, bitter and umami (a strong savoury taste like anchovies, soy sauce or a strong meaty broth) . Think of these words when you are identifying smells – can you describe the smell by categorising it into one of them? Try doing

{ The scent of your home should change and evolve with the seasons. }

this next time you eat an apple. Stop for a moment and smell it before you bite into it, breathing slowly. Train your nose. How does this smell make you feel? Raising your awareness of how smells affect you will help you become more in touch with your sense of smell, and how you can use it to change the feel of an environment.

After a while you should start to get a sense of your 'scent personality', what smells you are drawn to. Maybe you like floral notes but also the fresh zing of citrus. You might be drawn to muskier scents with deep woody undertones. Whatever it is, once you have figured out your scent personality you can use this to create a signature scent for your home. The goal is much like a signature perfume: every time someone smells it, it will remind them of you. Look at your notes, think of scents you are drawn to then think how you would recreate something that appeals to you. It is very

simple to combine essential oils and create your signature scent. You just need to play around a little.

I like a citrus scent with a spiced or musky undertone and a slight resinous top note – that could be made by combining essential oil of bergamot, petitgrain and wild rosemary. Another combination to create this would be mandarin, clove and eucalyptus. Put drops of your favourite oils together and create your favourite combination, remembering to jot down the quantities so you can recreate it.

You will also want to create different scents in different rooms and at different times of the day or year – the scent of your home should change and evolve with the seasons. For instance, a spring morning may call for geranium, citrus and other fresh and zingy notes that will make you feel alive and alert, while a winter's evening may be enhanced by the heady scent of myrrh, jasmine and frankincense: more grounding and calming smells. You can layer your scents by combining different candles and adding diffusers and room sprays, but be aware scent should be treated like sound, don't turn it up too loud. It should be a gentle background symphony rather than a room-filling screech of death metal.

Heavy scents will remain in the room for longer than citrus or light floral ones, so if you have a light, fresh room spray and an amber candle burning the effect will be one of initial fresh, floral ambience but lingering warmth and comfort as the evening goes on.

Essential Oils

Essential oils are concentrates that have been extracted from seeds, leaves, blossoms and other parts of plants. They are 50 to 70 times more intense than the plant in its natural state. Oils and herbs have been used for thousands of years for many beneficial reasons. They can be used in three ways: **aromatically**, **topically** and **internally**. Although completely natural, essential oils are powerful and should only be used internally under the guidance of an aromatherapist who has specialised training in the area.

Each individual oil has its own properties with different characteristics and healing actions. Once you become familiar with these different properties and, importantly, which scents resonate with you most, you will have an infinite list of combinations to use in your home and life. Their functions vary hugely – from calming and soothing to invigorating; from antifungal to antibacterial.

I have included many recipe combinations in the following chapters, but the most important thing is how you react to the smell – if you particularly are drawn to or repelled by a scent, then add or discard as desired. No matter what the qualities of a scent are believed to be, invigorating, calming or grounding is irrelevant if you do not find it pleasing.

Using Oils Aromatically

If you're starting out using essential oils and don't want to spend money yet on specialist diffusers, begin by just placing a few drops into a small bowl of hot water.

A simple ceramic diffuser in which you light a tea light is the next step up – these are really very cost-effective – you should be able to pick one up at your health food shop for around €15.

A plug-in diffuser is good if you are incorporating oils into your routine regularly, but don't get one that heats up as this changes the properties of the oils. *Muji* do really good and simple plug-in diffusers.

I recommend using no more than 8 to 10 drops of oil or blends at a time, in water or a diffuser, otherwise the smell can be too intense and cause headaches.

Using Oils Topically

Essential oils should never be applied neat to the skin as they can burn; they will need to be mixed with a carrier oil such as almond or olive oil. Each essential oil has its own list of properties. Below is just a small list of the essential oils available. I encourage you to go to your local health food shop and explore them for yourself.

Lavender	Antifungal, mildly sedative, calming and healing
Lemon	Antimicrobial, good for the circulation and a very fresh scent
Peppermint	Relieves headaches, good for digestion, invigorating
Tea tree	Antibacterial, antifungal, good for respiratory issues, insect repellent
Frankincense	Calming, quiets the mind, grounding, good for skin
Oregano	Antimicrobial, good for respiratory system
Clary sage	Helps with PMS, stress relief
Lemongrass	Relaxing, fresh-smelling, good for ligaments topically
Neroli	Antioxidant, stress relief, skin rejuvenation
Helichrysum	Healing
Cedarwood	Mild sedative, moth repellent
Rose	Calming, skin moisturiser
Vetiver	Calming, grounding
Ylang ylang	Promotes optimism, helps with courage
Bergamot	Relieves anxiety, calming
Chamomile	Mild sedative, calming
Eucalyptus	Aromatically a decongestant, relieves muscular pain
Rosemary	Helps with focus and concentration
Geranium	Antioxidant, topically helps tighten loose skin
Calendula	Anti-inflammatory, excellent for healing skin
Petitgrain	Promotes calm, eases tension, fosters skin health

Using Oils Internally

The truth is you already take essential oils internally – every time you chew a fresh herb or sprinkle cinnamon over something you eat you are ingesting the powerful properties contained within. That said, not all essential oils are safe to be taken internally and some, while safe in small doses, can cause irritation to your oesophagus or have other side effects. My advice if you are interested in exploring internal use of essential oils is to approach with caution and work with a health practictioner who can guide you.

Candles

I love a good scented candle. It's by far the most popular way to add scent to your home. The candles in my *Considered* range are among its most popular items and I use them throughout my house. There are a few tips that will help you get the best out of your candle.

Candle care

- Light candles an hour before you want peak scent
- Always wait until the wax pool reaches the edge of the candle before you blow it out, this prevents the centre of the candle burning down quicker than the surrounding area
- Always trim your wick to 5mm before you re-light it
- If you are burning a lot of candles, open your windows afterwards to clear the air.

The Air that You Breathe

Considering the amount of time we spend in our homes, it stands to reason that the air we breathe there should be as pure as possible. As well as smelling pleasant, it needs to be clean and free from pollutants. The strong, harsh smell of chemicals can linger and are certainly not the most pleasant scents to be inhaling as well as not being very good for your health. Keep the air in your home clean and fresh by following a few simple steps.

Open your windows. At least once a week, open all the windows in your house, creating a breeze and clearing stale air.

Switch to natural cleaners. I am not suggesting you bin those chemicals altogether (well, you might!) but that you become more mindful. A lot can be done with a lemon and some baking soda or plain hot, soapy water; also there are plenty of environmental choices in the supermarkets now (such as *Ecover*). As a start, try switching to natural products every *other* time you clean. You might just find that you are converted and with a little elbow grease your cupboard of chemicals can be greatly diminished.

Have many plants. Plants clean the air. Think of them as the lungs of your home, filtering the air and bringing in oxygen.

Smoke cleanse. The air in your home can hold negative energy. Medicinal smoke has been used for thousands of years to clear the air. The smoke cleanses the air of bacteria and the effects can last for up to one month. I like to do a smoke cleanse in my home at least every month, clearing the air of the past and getting ready for the new month ahead. To cleanse your air, select a smudge bundle of sage or a piece of palo santo. The latter is a South American wood belonging to the same family as myrrh and frankincense; it has medicinal properties and a unique smell. Smudge bundles are available in most health food shops, but you can also make your own by combining a bundle of herbs and drying them. Sage is the most common but rosemary, thyme and pine can also be used either on their own or combined together.

Open your windows to release the negative energy, light the bundle or palo santo over a candle, blow out the flame once it's taken, and allow it to

glow and burn. Resting it on a heat-proof plate or bowl, carry the smoking bundle around the area you wish to cleanse, paying attention to corners and areas where stagnant energy can accumulate. Once finished, allow the smoking bundle or wood to burn out or put it out in your heat-proof container. Do this any time you feel like your home needs a reset of energy. Never leave the bundle or wood unattended!

Make good environmental choices when decorating. Paint, carpets and furniture can all contain chemicals that leach into your air. Using natural materials wherever possible helps to keep negative chemicals out of the air.

Get some salt lamps. A Himalayan salt lamp is basically a large piece of pure Himalayan salt with a small bulb inside. It works by absorbing moisture and particles from the air such as dust, pollen, mould or mildew. When the water evaporates (emitting negative ions) the particles stay trapped in the salt. Have you ever gone for a brisk walk in the fresh air to clear your head? Well, that is exactly what negative ions do. By contrast, electronic devices give off positive ions which can make us feel tired and sluggish. Salt lamps are also said to help people with asthma and allergies. Start off with your bedroom, then, if you like it, install one or two (depending on room size) in your living room too. An added bonus is that they give off a lovely warm, soft light, are inexpensive and make a great night light in a small child's room. Most health food shops stock these lamps and they are also readily available online.

The Sound of Home

Do you know who is at your door simply by the way they ring the bell or knock? Do you have a memory of a squeaky bedroom door as a child? Sound can, like our other senses, stir memories, create calm or rouse irritation.

While we were filming the first RTÉ series of *Home of the Year*, on which I was a judge, we visited a house in Cork (that went on to win the competition). I will never forget walking into that home. It was on a very exposed location and it was a wild and blustery day. The wind was howling, but when we walked into the home and closed the door there was an incredible feeling of serenity and complete calm. Quickly I realised it was because the house was completely silent. It turned out this home was a passive house (very ecologically and energy-efficient) and was triple glazed, so as well as keeping heat in, it kept the sound of the howling winds out. The effect was quite dramatically soothing.

So can you use sound, or the minimising of negative sound in your home, to create the environment you want? Heavy curtains can help banish external noise pollution, so if you live near a busy road think about spending more on your curtains. Choose a heavy fabric or have them lined for extra sound protection.

{ Sound can, like our other senses, stir memories, create calm or rouse irritation. }

When you are choosing finishes for your floors, take into account who is living in your house. Wooden floors are beautiful of course, but being woken up at 3 am by teenagers traipsing up and down wooden stairs is not. Think about what effect the other finishes you are choosing will have on the noise in your home. Textiles and soft materials will act as sound absorbers, as will rugs, throws, carpets and cushions. This will be more important in some rooms such as the living room and especially bedrooms, where calm and tranquillity is essential. We don't necessarily need a quiet kitchen and this area may not have many textiles in it.

Make sure you fix any annoying noises in your home such as squeaky doors or buzzing or humming appliances. Sometimes you become used to something and don't realise it's been bothering you until it's gone. Just as negative energy can linger in your air, you can also do a sound cleanse in your home. If tensions are high or there has been some negative arguing or shouting, then a sound cleanse can reset the mood and energy. You can use a Tibetan meditation bowl, chimes or play some favourite music loudly, to fill the space with the positive sound vibrations. A positive sound has a positive effect on your mood.

The Tactile Home

The items that touch your body in your home should stimulate feelings of joy and comfort. Choose the best bed linen and towels you can afford and make sure they are 100 per cent natural fabrics. These are fabrics that touch your skin every day and nothing says comfort to me more than lying a newly bathed body down into a freshly made bed with crisp cotton sheets.

Aside from towels and bed linen, I favour natural fabrics everywhere in my home. Not only are they better for the environment, they also become more beautiful with age. A linen cloth that has been washed many times will be soft and tactile, worn wood tells a story of its past, as does a stone step with an indentation from many years of footsteps. Natural materials will hold their own and keep their dignity. They may cost more in the beginning but they are worth it in the long run: they will become examples of wabi-sabi at work (see page 22).

Texture can be a very useful tool when decorating your home. Think of texture as you would colour. You want to play with it – having all the same textures in a room will be just as bland as if you had all the same colour. Indeed, if you are limiting your palette, texture becomes even more important. You need to create contrasts:

- Plush velvet against a cool marble
- Metal and sheepskin
- Worn wood and deep-pile rug
- Gloss and matt – matt walls with gloss woodwork in the same hue.

Look at your home. Have you played with texture enough? Try adding something that plays and contrasts with what is already there. If you have a lot of hard, shiny surfaces like polished floors, tiles and metal then add some warmth and softness with woven baskets and textured rugs. The result will be instantaneous.

Materials for a sense of home

Below is a list of some of my favourite materials. I strongly favour natural fabrics and building materials. They are more distinguished, age more gracefully and are better for the environment.

Hard

Stone is long-lasting but expensive. Limestone, travertine and marble are all porous stones. They will need to be sealed and maintained. Granite and slate are more resilient and better for high-traffic areas like hallways.

Marble, technically a stone, deserves a unique mention. A small amount of marble can make any room look luxurious. Be careful if selecting marble for kitchens as it can damage easily. If you don't mind the wear and tear, then go for it. Marble is expensive though, so if decking out your entire bathroom is beyond your budget, go for accent pieces like marble accessories.

Wood, in the form of a solid wood floor, is a material that has gripped us in the most mainstream way in the last 20 years. Wood is also great as a kitchen counter. Vintage and weathered wood is an instant way to add texture and interest to a room.

Linoleum is having a bit of a comeback as it is available in a large variety of colours and is relatively inexpensive, hardwearing and easy to clean and maintain. Did you know it is actually made from linseed oil combined with cork dust, limestone and mineral pigments and so is also an eco-friendly option.

Cork provides eco-friendly flooring that is soft and warm underfoot. I laid a cork floor in my own home and loved it. It can also be dramatic as a wall covering in a bathroom or study.

Ceramic tiles are a great way to add colour. The handmade ones are incredibly beautiful but equally expensive.

Porcelain tiles are more expensive than ceramic as the dye seeps all the way through the tile, giving a richer colour.

Terracotta floor tiles are a go-to bathroom floor tile, they have a seventies vibe I like (think vintage *Habitat* catalogue) and a natural shading in the tiles which I also find appealing. Terracotta pots are also a favourite: exquisite in their simplicity.

Encaustic tiles are expensive but stunning. The pattern on these is made by colouring the clay and firing it so they have a real depth and are highly durable.

Brick is a great way to bring character to a new build. Look out for vintage bricks in salvage yards.

Brass has a warmth to it that stainless steel is lacking. A brass surround on a mirror or frame can add a nice dimension of texture. I love brass taps, but you need to accept that they will mark and stain.

Silver is something you can pick up in vintage form at flea markets and in junk shops. I like using vintage silver-plated cutlery every day, the weight is beautiful and it can be picked up at flea markets or junk shops for a good price. You can use old silver jugs and sugar bowls as containers for fresh flowers, don't worry about polishing them often, the patina is what makes them beautiful.

Soft

Linen is a fabric that will get better and better with age. Embrace the wrinkles. Look out for vintage linens in flea markets, mix your textures from fine to thick and slubby.

Cotton in its pure form is the only thing that should go on your bed (unless you are investing in linen sheets). Heavy cotton can also be used in rugs, curtains and cushions.

Wool, whether knitted or woven, is versatile and hardwearing for carpets, rugs, cushions, and more. You can use boiled wool as an upholstery fabric for a cosy effect with great durability.

Tweed is essentially wool, but woven into a tweed pattern (herringbone or twill). It can add a lovely masculine touch to a living room either by using a couple of throw cushions or covering an occasional chair or armchair.

Velvet and silk are great for adding texture and luxury, although they are generally not very hardwearing. It's best to use these in low-traffic areas such as the bedroom or on an occasional sofa.

Coir is made from the husk of coconuts so is very environmentally friendly. The only drawback is that it has a coarse texture so is not a good flooring choice for bathrooms or bedrooms where you might be walking barefoot. It is however perfect for doormats or mats in a mudroom or pantry.

Seagrass is a very durable material and naturally water repellent, making it good flooring for high-traffic areas such as hallways and stairs. Seagrass is also used to make baskets and containers and is a great material for adding texture.

Jute is used in rugs, it's very soft but not that durable. Use it in low-traffic areas like bedrooms.

Sisal is very coarse and though sturdy, can become slippery with wear and tear so is not suitable flooring for stairs. Sisal is also used in making rope and string.

Sheepskin, used as a rug, is something every home should have. It adds warmth and texture, has a very accessible price point and is portable.

Leather couches are the saviours of families everywhere. A good leather couch will stand an incredible amount of battering from small, sticky hands. Beware of new leather couches with rock-hard upholstery that are overstuffed. The leather should be soft and have removable seat cushions.

Books – the Heart of a Home

If plants are the lungs of your house, then books are its heart. A house with no books can feel sterile. Visually Books give a room texture and colour – all those coloured spines stretching along the shelf. I collect books, don't ask how many cookery books I have, I haven't counted and dare not. Books, to me, are magical and telling. They have informed my life. When I was frustrated with a career in the world of fashion that I no longer felt connected to, it was my bookshelf that led me in a new direction. I was taking 'time off' to have my third child and rethink what I was doing. It was 2008 and the world had basically gone belly up! I had been badly 'let down' by several clients. I realise everyone was desperately paddling to stay afloat, but for me, a sole trader supporting two and soon to be three children, this was the final moment in something that had long lost its appeal for me.

One day looking at my shelves, I realised that every book of non-fiction I owned was either a cookbook or one about homes and interiors. That was the steer I needed to redirect me. I decided there and then that my next step would involve either of these two passions, or if I could somehow wangle it … both.

Within two years I was beginning development of my brand *Considered* for Dunnes Stores, after taking a little pit stop back to New York along the way. My passion for books informed my decision to move into homewares and food. It helped me discover what my subconscious was telling me. A home without books feels cold and heartless to me and through my books I can trace the history of my adult life.

So now that you have a sense of what's involved in exploring your home anew, let's take a sensory journey through each room and discover simple and enjoyable ways to enhance your home, your tummy and, most importantly, your wellbeing.

The Flavour of Home

Is there anything that says 'home' more than food? We are, I believe, shaped by our culinary journey from birth onwards.

My path was somewhat unusual for a girl growing up in 1970s Ireland. Firstly, both of my parents are English, which immediately made me different. To be truthful, I didn't really identify with being Irish until I moved to New York City at the age of 23. On top of this my father was the Islamic curator at the Chester Beatty Library so my parents travelled extensively throughout the Middle East. I remember the excitement of them returning with large suitcases filled with sealed bags of pistachios, white knotted bags of dried limes (that to my small eyes looked like dusty golf balls), karkade (Egyptian hibiscus tea), which we would make into large vats of steaming purple tea and serve to visitors, eye-wateringly sweet halva, dried lemons and spices, powders and petals. They then would set about preparing incredible pots of steaming broths and stews. Lamb tagine, peshawari chicken and falafel were all regular midweek meals in my house. Of course, now in retrospect I can appreciate this and thank my parents for introducing me to such varied and enticing delicacies at a young age, but at the time I can remember begging my mother could we please eat 'normal' food!

By normal I meant the food that was eaten by the Griffins, the family of my best friend who lived across the road. The menu at the Griffin house could not have been more different. I can't really remember individual meals but I know there were a lot of boiled potatoes, the waxy kind that hold their shape and glisten so you can see every edge and turn of the knife that was used to peel them. There was meat, too, and certainly fish fingers but my favourite of all was the salad. This salad bore no resemblance at all to what was served in my house, which was a large wooden bowl of mixed leaves that appeared at every single meal we ever ate. I can clearly remember my mother asking, "Have you had some salad?", in fact she still makes a salad with every meal today and still asks the same question.

But no, in the Griffins', this was a plate with three lettuce leaves, a hard-boiled egg, a tomato that had been sliced into quarters, a slice of ham, pickled beetroot and my favourite addition, salad cream.

I think what I loved most of all about this meal was that it was self-contained, individualised, each person had their own plate with every item pre-prepared and served, there was something about this that so appealed to me. Meanwhile I would return to my own home (where couscous and tahini were staples) and dream of breaded chicken and over-boiled carrots.

It is something of a turn that now you cannot shake a marinated chicken stick in the air without hitting a bowl of hummus or a falafel. I am delighted as it means my favourite cuisine is available to me for breakfast, lunch and dinner in every format I could wish or imagine.

{ Food can stir up and create memories and emotion. }

Both of my parents come from the north of England (Yorkshire pudding is a competitive sport in our family!) and my grandparents on both sides were incredibly interested in food. Both grandfathers had impressive greenhouses where they grew tomatoes, grapes and lettuce as well as outdoor plots of carrots, courgettes and cabbage. I am assuming this was partly because they lived through the war and so self-sufficiency was a practical decision, but they kept it going for the rest of their lives and were incredibly proud of their produce. If my grandfathers' domain was their gardens, then my grandmothers' was most definitely the kitchen. Both were exceptional bakers and I have concluded that perhaps this gift skips a generation as none of their children are adept at baking at all (sorry, Mum).

My maternal grandmother was more of a savoury baker – her sausage rolls and meat pie were legendary. My father's mother was more of a sweet-toothed baker (although I can't say I ever saw her eat any of it). Every time we arrived to her house there would be a table laid with the same spread: coconut macaroons, biscuits, scones and *her* chocolate cake. As a late teenager I asked her for that cake recipe and she wrote it on a piece of paper, and it is a great sorrow to me that I, in standard teenage style, lost it.

A big part of my culinary development was the move to New York City in 1993. Apart from gaining at least a stone in weight within six months of arriving I was introduced to a whole new cupboard of foods including really, really good doughnuts, American pancakes with crispy bacon, proper Mexican food, sushi, pierogies and babka, which I would order at 3 am in *Odessa*, the best Polish diner on Tompkins Square, and eat, toasted and slathered in butter.

New York also stands out as it was the first time I really cooked for myself. I was in my early twenties and obsessed with *Vogue*, as I had been since I was 16 – I would walk across town every month to buy the British edition. But now my interest moved from the pages of dresses and make-up to include the food columnist who wrote about just the kind of things I wanted to eat. I soon became quite obsessed with her and her recipes. It helped that they were accompanied by fantastic illustrations. It was, of course, Nigella Lawson. I tore out her monthly column and kept a blue folder with the recipes in it for years. Her first book *How to Eat* became my bible – my copy, which has survived three moves across the Atlantic, now has no cover at all and looks like it has been run over multiple times, but they are the scars of love and much usage.

So really my taste in food is a product of all of this, of my life, and I haven't even mentioned summers spent in Spain, picking figs and making jam, and glorious days in west Cork eating just-caught mackerel barbecued on the beach.

Food can stir up and create memories and emotion.

Isn't this what you want to create in your home?

A Note about the Recipes in this Book

I would like to say I eat a balanced diet and this is true, but the balance seems to come in great waves and surges. As I have increased in age and wisdom (yes, it's true), I have been able to extend the bouts of green, and decrease the weekends of crunchy, sugary treats – it's a work in progress. I am also very interested in what is going on in the food world so, yes, clean eating and gut health are all areas I have spent a lot of time discovering, but I will always enjoy a slice of cake or a perfect scone, because they taste delicious. They are healthy to me because they gladden my heart and warm my soul and what could be better than that? The recipes are divided room by room – with homemade beauty and bath products for bathroom. From informal dining to TV dinners to the perfect bedrom feast, there's something for every occasion – and they are grouped at the end of each chapter.

I am not condoning this way of eating, nor preaching any particular family of food or style of diet; I am simply stating it as what *I* do. I love to bake for therapy and meditation. I also go through phases of complete obsession (this also happens with lunch destinations and songs). I might be on a shortbread wave and make nothing but shortbread and its variations for weeks, slightly tweaking flours, sugar content, additions. As a result, I have firm recipe favourites that I can defend because I have tested and tasted their competitors. This does not mean though that they cannot be knocked off the spot, and other contenders can become the number one at any given time.

So the recipes in this book are favourites.

They are the food I cook and have cooked, the recipes I bake.

They are, for me . . . a sense of home.

Notes

Flour is always plain unless otherwise stated.

Butter is always salted unless stated.

Salt is always sea salt or Himalayan.

Eggs are always free range and preferably organic, medium size.

Honey is raw (unless you are cooking with it). Raw honey is full of vitamins and enzymes. It is unheated and unpasteurised. It is a food that becomes alkaline in the digestive tract and so can relieve nausea and the enzymes can help you digest other foods. When using raw honey you must not heat it above body temperature or you will destroy the beneficial properties. It will still taste delicious though.

Kitchen

I find refuge in my kitchen.

OUR ATTITUDE to the kitchen has changed so much, maybe more than to any other room in the house. A kitchen was once something that was seen as being purely functional, something to be hidden away in the basement. Now we see it as being the heart of the home and therefore one of the most important rooms in the house. Despite this shift, many people still treat the kitchen as a purely utilitarian room – one where you prepare food, cook, clean and wash – thus neglecting the important qualities of beauty and atmosphere. There are many things that you can do to make the kitchen feel inviting and cosy, a place to indulge each of your senses – from the particular touch of your kitchen table, the colours on the walls, to the smell and taste of the food that you eat.

I find refuge in my kitchen and often turn to it for two of my favourite pursuits, cooking and baking, particularly if I am stressed. When I moved back to New York seven years ago, baking was one of the things I really missed about living in rural Ireland. While I had a kitchen in New York, it just wasn't a very pleasant place to hang out – it was very small and the window looked out onto somebody else's terrace. Also I was too busy to bake (well, you just always seem to be busier in New York). At the very time I needed respite I was too busy to find it in one of the places it has always been for me: the kitchen. So on my return to Ireland, baking and the kitchen view onto my garden were the two things that I never again took for granted.

The Look and Feel of Your Kitchen

The big-ticket items in your kitchen are the kitchen units. Custom-built kitchens can run into the tens of thousands so if your budget doesn't stretch to that, what can you do to give your kitchen the appeal and sensuality you want? Plain wooden shaker-style kitchens are one of my favourite choices as they make sense on so many levels. They are timeless, functional and you can choose from a huge variety of colours and handles. Then you can update both of these at a later date for a whole new look, at minimal expenditure. A solid wood kitchen will pay off in the long run in quality and durability. When looking at colours try to push the boundary a little – if you really want a white or grey then go for something with warmth: a white with a hint of pink or green or a grey with a blue undertone. A contrasting trim can add a touch of drama; a kitchen painted all over in one colour can be very chic and modern-looking. Whatever palette you go for, remember if you are relying heavily on neutrals you will need to pay attention to texture. Marble, stone, wood, brass, natural-fibre rugs, baskets and even stainless steel counters can all be incorporated and bring a variety of surfaces and interest.

Another option is to buy the carcass of the kitchen off the shelf and have custom doors made. This means you can choose a more expensive or unusual finish. Weathered wood looks amazing made into cabinet doors and adds a unique warmth and texture. Look in salvage yards for old boards – you may find some that are beautiful and in short supply, so therefore a good price, just enough to fashion some cupboard doors.

Door handles are the jewellery of your room and the perfect opportunity to add your own touch. A very plain fitted kitchen can be made to look much more expensive by adding good-quality handles and it is also a way to update a tired-looking kitchen. Think outside of traditional offers and scour the high street for quirky animal heads, brass insects, porcelain or glass handles. This is an instant update and adds real charm and whimsy something lacking in many kitchens. Flea markets and junk shops are also a great resource for handles. Personally I love brass handles but if you favour silver why not try a nickel finish instead of stainless steel. It has a much warmer tone. Whatever you choose, my advice is to match it to your taps, much like wearing gold earrings and rings at the same time, a mix of metals can look muddled and uncoordinated, matching them will make for a much more harmonious feel.

Your kitchen taps work hard for a living – you use them every day, so here is not the place to cut corners on quality. There are so many different designs available but below are the basic types that you will encounter. Most designs will come with three choices of handle: knob, crosshead and lever. The choice of handle is really up to personal taste and will not affect performance.

1. **Pillar taps** are two separate taps for hot and cold water and require two holes drilled into your worktop. They are not so popular now and are quite a traditional choice, but they work well if you have a very traditional kitchen and want to keep the look consistent.

2. **A mixer tap** has one spout with two separate taps. It requires two or three holes to be drilled in your worktop, depending on design. It is a good basic choice with multiple designs available, including a bridge mixer which lifts the centre bar off the worktop and mixes water before it enters the spout.

3. **Monoblanc** is a more minimalist-looking tap than a mixer, with only one drill hole required. There are two taps either side and a mixer spout. It's a very good well-functioning type of tap.

4. **A single lever tap** requires one hole in the worktop and is a very streamlined option. Personally I am not a big fan and prefer my hot and cold water to be served by individual taps

5. **Wall-mounted taps** are great if you are short on space or dealing with a narrow kitchen. They also eliminate the problem of cleaning around your taps on your worktop.

6. **Pull-out spray taps** were originally designed for commercial kitchens and involve a tap on some kind of hose that can be extended to rinse dishes or vegetables – handy if you have a double sink, cook a lot or have a big family. The original designs take up space but there are newer types where the hose retracts beneath your worktop. This is a sleeker option, particularly in a smaller space.

The other big decision unique to your kitchen is your choice of worktop. In fulfilling all its necessary roles, it may be scratched, pounded, cut, scrubbed, stained and subjected to extreme temperatures. You need to ask yourself who will be using the kitchen – if you have a clatter of teenagers in the house, anything high-maintenance or easily stained is a no-go. How much upkeep are you willing to do? Most natural materials like wood or stone will require some kind of upkeep, oiling for wood and applying a sealant for stone. Are you committed to this? If not, then think about an alternative surface like corian or stainless steel. What is your surface area and budget? If you have a large surface area and small budget, then high-end finishes like marble will be ruled out. If your heart is set on a Carrara marble counter, however, that will make your heart dance every time you see it, can you stretch your budget here and save somewhere else? Or can you use it in a part of the space, even the backsplash? Beware, though, of using different materials in small amounts – this just ends up looking bitty and cheap. Commit to your choice and follow through, being as bold as your budget allows. As a general rule, a material should be used all the way to its natural boundary line, so the edge of the room for the floor, the end of the wall or shelving/cabinets for tiles.

I know the fashion at the moment is for open-plan kitchens – everyone is knocking down walls and removing doors. Personally I prefer rooms, a bit of privacy. Now, I understand you may have small children and want to keep your eye on them when cooking, but sometimes walking into the kitchen, switching on your favourite tune and cooking a meal with no distractions can be better than a therapy session. Open-plan or a room on its own though, don't forget about the personality of your kitchen, *your* personality.

Most of my favourite kitchen spaces have some free-standing furniture in them: an over-fitted kitchen can look bland and heartless. Look for old pieces that can function well in your kitchen and bring charisma and flair to break up the clinical look of a completely built-in kitchen. Examples could be an oak dresser or an old sideboard (wood can be painted or stripped to your taste). Your kitchen island could be a reconditioned workbench or

vintage table. If like me you have a bit of a cookery book addiction, then a bookshelf to house all of your cookery books is a practical option. Have a rethink about over-the-counter cabinets. Could you live without them? Or substitute with open shelving above the counter? This is a growing trend as people find over-the-counter cabinets suddenly feel slightly old-fashioned and heavy, while open shelving really helps to make the kitchen feel more relaxed. Place the items you use every day, such as certain mixing or serving bowls, on your open shelves – this way they won't get dusty and it's a great way to make you edit your cupboards. Place a long hanging bar underneath to hang utensils and kitchen tea towels.

{ Most of my favourite kitchen spaces have some free-standing furniture in them. }

Flooring in a kitchen needs to be highly functional so anything with crevices or holes (such as a naturally finished travertine) is best avoided. I do like the idea of a wooden floor in a kitchen though, it adds warmth to this space. Cork is also a fantastic option – durable, soft underfoot and easy to maintain. Tiles on kitchen floors can look rather cold but if I was going to choose a type, I would opt for terracotta.

Remember to hang pictures in your kitchen to make it feel like an important part of your home. As this is a room where you spend a lot of time, it should feel comfortable and inviting. I also love to put up decorative trays on the kitchen wall. Stick them onto the walls with those little double-sided Velcro strips. Then you can simply un-Velcro them when you want to use them and stick them back up on the wall when you're done.

The Science of a Perfect Kitchen Design

If you are designing a kitchen from scratch, then there are some measurements that you should take into consideration.

- The work aisle, where you stand to prepare food, should ideally be 106cm wide and walkway width should be a minimum of 90cm.
- The standard countertop height is 92cm high and 64cm deep.
- An upper cabinet is 30cm deep.
- If you have a centre island with a pendant light, then ideally there should be 76cm between the pendant and your island.

These are industry norms, though if you are having a custom kitchen built (lucky you!) and you are exceptionally tall or smaller than the norm you can of course adjust the heights to suit, but remember you may not be the only person ever to cook in the kitchen. Generally, these standard heights work for most people.

A SENSE OF HOME

Lighting for an Effective – and Beautiful – Space

The lighting in your kitchen needs to be functional above all, and will depend on your space and how you use it. Task lighting is very important: place overhead lights in front of where you stand at your worktop, so they do not cast a shadow on your counter. Remember to also add ambient lighting, particularly if you eat in your kitchen. A table lamp is a lovely and unexpected addition to your counter, your kitchen table or on top of your dresser.

Lighting under your top cabinets is very effective.

A Scented Kitchen

Most of the smells in your kitchen will come from the delicious food you are cooking there. You can't beat the aroma of freshly baked bread, just-out-of-the-oven chocolate cake or a batch of hot scones waiting to be buttered. However, not all cooking smells fragrant after the event – frying anything can leave a lingering bad smell as can fish, cauliflower, or delicious but maybe not so pleasant-smelling cheese!

Baking soda and vinegar are both wonderful odour absorbers. Placing a jar of baking soda in your fridge will soak up any unwanted smells caused by strong-smelling food in there. For your counter top, pour some baking soda into a jar, add some sprigs of woody herbs like rosemary or bay and top with a piece of hessian or muslin tied with string. This works great to absorb odours present in the air.

Every kitchen needs fresh herbs and they are so easy to buy now, no one really has an excuse not to have them to hand every day. Think of the smell of a freshly rubbed leaf of, say, rosemary or thyme between your fingers – it's such an invigorating scent and gets your olfactory senses buzzing.

While it is a good idea to grow the herbs you use most often, it is also fun to grow more unusual plants that can be difficult to get fresh from normal shops. These are my top fresh herbs to have in (or near) the kitchen.

- Coriander
- Dill
- Thyme
- Bay
- Lemon verbena
- Lemon balm
- Lemongrass
- Thai basil
- Mint (specifically apple mint)
- Flat-leaf parsley
- Fennel
- Curry tree
- Kaffir lime

If you have an abundance of herbs at any one time you can freeze them in olive oil ready for future use. Simply place small amounts of herbs into an ice cube tray, pour over some olive oil and freeze until solid, then pop them

out and transfer to a labelled freezer bag. Add a cube to your cooking pan when you want to use.

Homemade Cleaning

Have you noticed that the kitchen is the room where you seem to do the most cleaning? How many times today have you squirted that brightly coloured bottle of multi-action spray from the supermarket on your surfaces? It's no surprise – here is where we are constantly preparing food, then clearing it up, and around food, it's vitally important to have cleanliness, freshness, and no nasty odours. We all want to use fewer chemical products to conserve our planet (and health), so switching to natural cleaning products in the kitchen makes sense. Be open-minded – you'll be surprised by how effective these are. The trick to using natural cleaners is not to let the grime build up too much. Little and often is the mantra. Here are some tips and recipes for natural cleaning – not just for your kitchen, but for your whole home.

Cups

Remove tea and coffee stains from cups by soaking them in a solution of 1 part baking soda and 2 parts water for 2 hours. For very stubborn stains, soak overnight.

Pans

For burned pans sprinkle the area with baking soda and add cold water. Let it sit overnight if necessary, then scrub away in the morning.

Glassware

Add 1 cup of distilled vinegar to your dishwasher to remove clouded stains from glasses. Either put in the rinse aid compartment or directly into the bottom of your dishwasher before you run the cycle.

Wooden Worktops

Sprinkle the worktop with salt and then use half a lemon to rub the salt all over the surface. Leave for half an hour then rinse with warm water and wipe dry immediately.

Silver Cleaning

This method is magic – it takes all the heavy scrubbing out of the silver-cleaning process. For small items like cutlery or jewellery, you can use a smallish plastic, glass or ceramic container. For larger items such as bowls and teapots, you can use your kitchen sink.

- Line the bottom of the container or sink with tin foil, shiny side-up.
- Place your silver items on the foil.
- Sprinkle liberally with baking soda.
- Add enough boiling water to completely cover the items.
- Leave until the water is cool enough to scoop out the items with your hands – you should be able to see them change colour and brighten up before your eyes!
- Buff with a soft cloth until shiny and dry.

Surface Cleaner

2 cups water
½ cup white vinegar
1 teaspoon washing-up liquid
1 tablespoon baking soda

Combine all ingredients in a clean spray bottle and shake. Spray onto surfaces and wipe clean. Note: This is not suitable for marble or travertine surfaces.

Kitchen Recipes

Classic Tastes

There are some recipes that every baker/cook should have in their repertoire. The classics, the bedrock of many meals, recipes you fall back on again and again and adapt. You may have made them originally because you were inspired by a meal in a restaurant or while looking through a cookbook, then made them your own. I believe that a recipe is an organic thing, something that changes and grows with you as you grow and change as a cook. Every one of the recipes below means something to me. Whether they are the go-to cake I have always made for my children's birthdays or the fall-back roast for many a special occasion, they are the recipes I use time and again for entertaining, therapy and meditation, constantly tweaking, altering, adding or subtracting. This is my personal repertoire – the recipes I would like to pass on to my children and grandchildren, as my grandparents passed their recipes on to me. They are listed in no particular order.

- Great White Loaf
- Just the Best Chocolate Chip Cookies
- Oh So Simple Pastry Case
- Holy Moly Chocolate Brownies
- Shortbread that Crumbles and Melts in Your Mouth
- Mood-altering Salad Dressing
- Not My Grandmother's Chocolate Cake
- You're Such a Flake Flaky Pastry
- Basic Rich Tomato Sauce
- Loaf Cake, Maybe Lemon
- Soul Chicken Stock
- Roast Leg of Lamb
- Homemade Pizza That Is Actually Good

Great White Loaf

This is one of the most important recipes in my whole repertoire, not because it produces a great loaf of crusty white bread with a soft chewy centre, which it also does, but because it altered my relationship with yeast irrevocably.

It may seem strange to weigh your liquid but this is common in bread-making as it gives you a more accurate amount. Be aware that you will be baking this bread 18 to 24 hours after you begin it, so decide when you want to eat it and work back. You will need a heavy-cast iron pot (6–8 litres) with a lid.

Makes 1 large loaf

430g flour (strong white is best but plain flour will also work
    if that's all you have)
7g yeast
2 teaspoons sea salt
345 grams water

Measure out your flour and place into a very large bowl, big enough to hold double the amount of the mixture (as it will more than double in size). Add the yeast and salt and stir with your clean hands, then add the water and also mix with your hands until you have a shaggy, wet dough.

Mix until it comes together into one mass, cover the bowl with cling film and place somewhere cool for 18 to 24 hours.

An hour before you are ready to bake turn your oven to its highest setting, which is usually somewhere around 250°C. Place the pot in the oven to heat up (without the lid).

Turn out your dough onto a floured worktop and gather the edges into the centre to create a round ball, then flip the dough over so the seam is at the bottom and you have a smooth round surface on top.

After 45 minutes to an hour remove your pot from the oven – take care as it will be extremely hot. Carefully transfer the dough to the pot, keeping the seam at the bottom, then make a few slashes in the top with a very sharp knife. Place the lid on, put in the oven and bake for 35–45 minutes. The lidded pot creates a steamy environment which gives that delicious toffee-coloured chewy crust.

Remove the lid and bake for a further 10 to 15 minutes (approx. 1 hour cooking time in total). When done, the top should be brown and the bottom should sound hollow when tapped. Remove from the oven and allow to cool completely before cutting. Needless to say it's best eaten straight away but does make exceptional toast the next day and a few days after.

Just the Best Chocolate Chip Cookies

When I lived in Brooklyn in 2010 I ate a cookie in a small café on Smith Street. It was large and caramel-coloured with big chocolate chunks, crispy edges and a soft, chewy centre. I fell in love instantly, and even though this café was further from my house than was necessary to walk for a good cup of coffee I made it my Saturday morning ritual to go there, sometimes buying three cookies to see me through the weekend.

This recipe, based on the New York Times 48-hour cookie, is the closest thing I have found to that heavenly specimen. You can wait anything between 24 to 48 hours to bake these – the longer you wait, the richer and more caramelised the cookie will taste. My personal preference is somewhere around the 36-hour mark. Don't substitute chocolate chips here, you want good-quality chocolate broken into chunks, at least thumbnail size. This will affect the taste but also the texture of your cookie. These cookies can be frozen once they've had their waiting time – just defrost at room temperature before you bake. Do not skip the stage of weighing out the cookie dough! As with all my recipes, I have made this the shortest route to the desired effect.

Makes 18 cookies

480g plain flour
1 ¼ teaspoons baking soda
1 ½ teaspoons baking powder
1 ½ teaspoons sea salt
280g unsalted butter
280g light brown sugar
200g caster sugar
2 free-range eggs
200g dark chocolate (60–70%), roughly broken into chunks

Measure the flour, baking soda, baking powder and salt into a bowl and stir with a whisk to remove any lumps. In a separate bowl, cream the butter and both sugars together until pale and light, about 5 minutes. Add the eggs one at a time, mixing well between each addition.

Add the flour mixture to the bowl and mix until well combined (don't over-mix). Add the chocolate chunks and mix through. Now, fashion golf ball-sized rounds of the dough with your hands (each one should weigh 100g). Cover the bowl of dough balls with cling film and put in the fridge for 24 to 36 hours.

When you are ready to bake, place the cookie balls on baking trays lined with parchment paper, leaving plenty of space between each one – I find four cookies a sheet works well if you don't want them to melt into one another. Allow to come to room temperature (about half an hour) while you preheat your oven to 180°C. Bake for 18 to 20 minutes until golden brown. Remove from the oven and allow to cool on the tray.

These cookies are best the day they come out of the oven but if kept in a completely airtight container will last up to three days.

Oh So Simple Pastry Case

I first came across this pastry case on the blog of American pastry chef David Lebovitz. It was certainly a revelation to me. No chilling the dough, no carefully rolling out the pastry and transferring it to the case, no blind baking and cooling. You just place the ingredients in the oven, stir and press into a dish. The results are divine: a slightly caramel-flavoured pastry case that is dry and crumbly. You can fill it with a multitude of options such as chopped apricots tossed in lemon juice and a spoonful of sugar, spread with jam and a frangipane, or pecans or other nuts.

180g butter cut into cubes

2 tablespoon plain oil (sunflower or canola)

6 tablespoons water

2 tablespoons caster sugar

¼ teaspoon sea salt

300g plain flour

Preheat the oven to 180°C. Place the butter, oil, water, sugar and salt in a medium-size ovenproof ceramic or pyrex dish (not metal). You do not need to combine or mix, just pop them all on top of each other.

Place the dish in the oven for 15 minutes or until the butter has melted and is starting to bubble and brown at the edges.

Remove from the oven and pour in the flour (be careful as contents will be hot). Stir vigorously until the dough comes together and starts to pull away from the sides. Allow to cool for a minute or two and then transfer to a tart tin. Press into the base and sides until smooth and even, reserving a little piece of the dough to fill in any cracks.

Prick the dough all over with a fork and bake for 15 minutes. Remove from the oven, fill with the filling of choice and bake for 30 minutes more or as directed.

Holy Moly Chocolate Brownies

If I'm going to eat a brownie, then I make it the best brownie I can possibly eat. I'm not wasting that indulgence on something dry or tasteless. I want something moist and fudge-like with large chunks of chocolate. This is my ultimate brownie recipe, adjusted to my personal idea of perfection. Use whatever chocolate you like, but remember milk chocolate has more sugar so you may want to add less. Make sure you get a good frothy, pale consistency when you are whisking your eggs and sugar – this step creates the thin crust on top and the slight chew in the texture of the brownies. DO NOT overcook these – you want the centre to be gooey when you take it out of the oven. I prefer my brownies without nuts but if you would rather add them I would recommend adding a handful of pecans or possibly toasted hazelnuts.

Makes 16–32 brownies, depending on how much of a sugar rush you want

250g butter

200g caster sugar

200g light brown sugar

4 free-range eggs

2 teaspoons vanilla extract

75g plain flour

75g cocoa

1 teaspoon baking powder

300g dark chocolate

(60%–70%), broken into chunks

Preheat the oven to 180°C and grease and line a baking tin (about 20 x 25 cm) with baking parchment.

Melt the butter, either in a pan or in your microwave. Put the eggs and sugars into a large bowl and whisk together until pale, light and frothy, about 3 to 5 minutes.

Add the slightly cooled butter and vanilla extract to the egg mixture and gently stir a couple of times.

Sift in the flour, cocoa and baking powder, then fold into the mixture, being careful not to over-mix. Gently stir in the chocolate chunks.

Pour the mixture into the prepared tin, smoothing the top. Bake for 30 minutes until a crust forms on the top and the centre is gooey but not wet. Remove and leave to cool in the tin before cutting into squares.

Shortbread that Crumbles and Melts in Your Mouth

Shortbread is the first thing I ever baked. When I was a child my mother had a large black tome of a cookery book. It had been a wedding present and was the kind of gift that was given to a young woman by her mother as she set off to make her own home. I seem to recall that I made shortbread because the list of ingredients was very short and the method seemed quite simple. It began my love affair with baking and pretty soon I was making shortbread regularly and gifting it to friends, sometimes with the ends dipped in melted chocolate and presented in old tea boxes meticulously covered in tin foil. The recipe and method has greatly evolved since those early days and this is probably one of the recipes I make most often and is often requested by visiting friends. The baking method may seem a little complex but I promise this will yield the crumbliest and most mouth-melty shortbread possible. Allowing it to cool in the warm oven dries it out and gives it the amazing texture, but I have been known to sneak one piece out and eat it while it was still hot, burning my lips and letting it crumble down my apron …

Makes about 12 biscuits

60g rolled oats
180g plain flour
60g cornflour
100g caster sugar plus 2 tablespoons for top
½ teaspoon sea salt
200g butter (cold and cut into cubes)

Place your oats into a grinder or food processor and pulse until you have a fine flour. Pour into a bowl and add the remaining dry ingredients and stir.

Now add the butter and rub in with your fingers to become like breadcrumbs. Continue until it comes together into a dough, being careful not to over-mix.

Transfer the dough onto a sheet of baking parchment and bring together into a mound, pressing firmly to bring any stray pieces in. Shape the dough into a long log shape, roughly 16 x 6cm and flatten each end. Wrap in the parchment paper and roll it to make it nice and even and round. Place in the fridge for at least an hour.

Preheat your oven to 180°C. Remove the dough from the fridge and cut the log into 1½cm-thick biscuits. Transfer to a lined baking sheet and put in the oven for 30 minutes, after 30 minutes slide out the tray and sprinkle over the 2 tablespoons of sugar, slide shortbread back in. Turn the oven off, leave the door slightly ajar and allow the biscuits to cool for at least half an hour in the oven.

Optional flavours to add to these biscuits:
You can add flavours to these cookies – just put them in at the 'breadcrumb' stage and rub in with your hands. Here are some of my favourite combinations.

Chocolate and Hazelnut

100g chocolate chunks, chopped small
50g toasted hazelnuts, slightly crumbled

Stem Ginger

80g crystallised ginger, chopped fine
1 teaspoon freshly ground ginger root

Oranges and Lemons

Zest of 1 orange and 1 lemon

Lemon and Cardamom

Zest of 1 lemon
Seeds from 3–4 cardamom pods, lightly crushed

Mood-altering Salad Dressing

So turmeric is all the rage. Antioxidant and anti-inflammatory, it's claimed to be so good for you. Though I'm all for eating to boost your immune system and like the idea of food as medicine and mood enhancers, if it doesn't taste good, then it doesn't make its way into my kitchen or my belly.

I created this recipe while trying to add more turmeric into my everyday diet. It has omega 3s from the olive oil, apple cider vinegar which is full of gut-friendly bacteria, raw honey which is full of nutrients and beneficial enzymes, fresh ginger which is calming for your digestive tract and garlic which is great for your immune system. The black pepper is said to help your body absorb the benefits of the turmeric. But most importantly, it tastes absolutely delicious. I like to use fresh turmeric which is now available in most supermarkets and health food shops as the taste is much more mellow, but dried will also work fine. Excellent over a green salad but equally tasty over grains or roasted vegetables.

1 teaspoon grated fresh turmeric/ground turmeric
1 teaspoon fresh ginger (grated)
1 clove of garlic (crushed)
1 tablespoon raw honey
3 tablespoons extra virgin olive oil
1 tablespoon apple cider vinegar
a grind of fresh black pepper

Simply blend all the ingredients together and use. If you have extra it will store in a jar in the fridge for 1 to 2 weeks.

Not My Grandmother's Chocolate Cake

It would be fair to say I bake a lot! People often say to me, "Your kids are so lucky, they must be delighted to be always getting freshly baked cakes, breads and cookies." The reality is they really don't pay much attention to it, in fact they often give me a hard time for trying out some new flavour combination involving flowers or spices that they find unappealing. However, the first time I made this cake my eldest son Obi took a bite and exclaimed a single word: "Finally!" Rare praise indeed. As I mentioned, my paternal grandmother was a great baker and she did indeed give me the recipe for her chocolate cake when I was about 18, but I subsequently lost it somewhere along the way in all my various moves around the world and Ireland. So this is not her recipe, but somehow it feels right to mention her and dedicate a chocolate cake to her, as I will always associate it with her. This unbelievably moist, light and not too sweet cake is perfect for a birthday cake, or simply afternoon tea.

200g butter	300g caster sugar
125ml milk	¼ teaspoon sea salt
240g plain flour	2 free-range eggs
1½ teaspoons baking soda	100ml double cream
70g cocoa	100ml hot coffee

For the chocolate buttercream:
260g butter (softened)
150g icing sugar
100g chocolate (60% cocoa solids) roughly chopped

For the chocolate topping:
100g chocolate (60% cocoa solids) roughly chopped
80g cold butter

Preheat the oven to 180°C. Butter, flour and line the bases of two 15cm cake tins with baking parchment.

Place the butter and milk into a saucepan over a medium heat until butter melts, then set aside to cool. In a large bowl combine the flour, baking soda, cocoa, sugar and salt, and mix until completely combined. Add the cooled butter and milk mixture and stir. Add the eggs and cream and mix well, then pour in the hot coffee and stir, to give a fairly loose consistency of batter.

Divide the batter between the two tins and bake for 35 to 40 minutes or until a knife comes out clean when tested. Leave in the tin to cool for 10 minutes then turn onto a wire rack to cool fully.

While the cake is baking make the chocolate buttercream. Place the butter (minus 2 tablespoons) in a bowl and whisk until pale and soft, then sift in the icing sugar and whisk again.

Place the chocolate and 2 tablespoons of butter in a pan over a very low heat. Stir and remove from heat before the chocolate is completely melted. Continue stirring until chocolate is totally smooth. Pour the melted chocolate into the whipped butter continually whisking. Set aside.

To make the topping, place the roughly chopped chocolate and 30g of the butter into a pan over a low heat. Remove before the chocolate has completely melted and some is still solid. Stir off the heat until smooth. Add the remaining cold butter and stir vigorously until the butter has melted and you have a thick, silky mixture. Adding the *cold* butter to the *hot* chocolate mixture is what makes the topping extra-shiny and glossy.

To assemble the cake:
When your cakes are cooled, place one cake layer on a plate or cake-stand, smooth over with one-third of the buttercream, place the other cake on top and cover the top with another third of buttercream. Slather the remaining third around the edges. Chill for 15 minutes, remove from fridge and pour over the chocolate topping, letting some of it drip down the sides. This cake will keep for 2 to 3 days in an airtight container, if it lasts that long!

You're Such a Flake Flaky Pastry

This is a perfect flaky pastry – excellent for a sweet or a savoury pie. There are a couple of things you want to pay attention to here.

1. Make sure all your ingredients are *really* cold, you can even pop your flour into the fridge for an hour in the bowl before you begin. And make sure the water is ICE cold.

2. Leave lots of large lumps of butter – they should be bigger than pea-sized. These butter lumps are what make your pastry super-flaky!

Makes 2 x 23cm crusts

320g plain flour
a pinch of sea salt
230g cold butter, half of it cubed and half of it sliced into long, thin strips
120ml iced water
1 free-range egg, beaten

It is best to make this pastry by hand so you can control the size of the butter lumps. Place the flour and salt in a large bowl and stir lightly with your clean hands to blend and remove any lumps. Add the cold butter and rub with your hands until the butter begins to incorporate, but you still have large lumps the size of almonds.

Add the iced water 1 tablespoon at a time, mixing lightly with your hands between each addition. After you have added all the water tip the mixture onto a lightly floured worktop and bring together. Flatten into a large square about 10 x 10cm then cut into quarters. Put each quarter one on top of the other and flatten again to a large square. Divide into two discs, wrap in cling film and refrigerate for at least half an hour.

When you are ready to use, roll one of the pastry discs to be larger than the circumference of your pie dish and carefully lift it on, gently easing it into the edges. Refrigerate again for at least an hour before baking – it's the cold crust going into a hot oven that will produce the flake you desire.

When you are ready to bake, heat your oven to 220°C and roll the second pastry disc into a circle. Now take out the pie crust from the fridge, add your desired filling and place the second crust on top. Pinch the edges to clamp them together. Cut four vents in the top of the pie dough and brush with the beaten egg. If your kitchen is very hot you can place the pie back in the fridge for 10 minutes before putting it in the oven.

Bake for 15 minutes then reduce the heat to 180°C; continue baking for 30 to 40 minutes until golden.

A note on fillings:
This pie is perfect for any fruit fillings. As a general rule you will need 700 to 800g of fruit, 2 tablespoons of sugar, the juice of half a lemon and 2 tablespoons of cornflour to fill this pie. Try peaches, plums, nectarines, blueberries, strawberries, blackberries or a combination like peach and strawberry or plum and blackberry. Just toss the fruit into a bowl (chop peaches, nectarines and plums into eighths), sprinkle the sugar, cornflour and lemon juice on top and stir before tipping into the cold uncooked crust.

Allow your pie to cool to room temperature before eating.

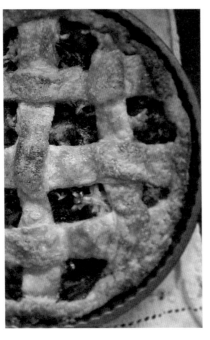

Basic Rich Tomato Sauce

A good tomato sauce is the basis for so many dishes. Eaten simply tossed through some freshly cooked pasta, spread on your homemade pizza or as the base of good stew, this sauce combines roasted tomatoes with tinned to give a really rich, flavoursome combination. The trick of browning the garlic comes from the wonderful chef April Bloomfield who I had the pleasure to meet at Ballymaloe a couple of years ago. Make a large batch and freeze it so you always have it on hand. As the tomatoes take 2 hours to roast, you'll need to start this sauce well in advance of when you want to use it.

Makes about 1 litre

1 medium onion
600g cherry tomatoes
1–2 teaspoons sea salt
a sprig of fresh thyme and oregano
2 tablespoons olive oil
1 tablespoon balsamic vinegar
2 x 400g good-quality tins of whole tomatoes
2 cloves of garlic, peeled and thinly sliced

Preheat the oven to 100°C. Peel the onion, chop into quarters and separate the layers so that you have 1 or 2 layers of onion and they are not all stuck together. Toss the cherry tomatoes and chopped onion into a large roasting pan and sprinkle with 1 teaspoon of sea salt, the fresh herbs, a tablespoon of olive oil and the balsamic vinegar. Place in the oven and leave to slowly roast for 2 hours.

While the cherry tomatoes are roasting drain the 2 tins of tomatoes and set the liquid aside. Reach into the sieve and squish the tomatoes up, breaking them into small pieces and draining off excess liquid.

When the cherry tomatoes are ready place a pan on the hob with a tablespoon of olive oil, add the garlic and fry until it just starts to turn brown. Be careful not to burn it or it will taste bitter and acrid. Add the tomatoes from the sieve and stir for 2 to 3 minutes, breaking them up with a wooden spoon until the sauce comes together into one mass. Add the roasted cherry tomatoes and onions and pour over the reserved tomato liquid. Stir with your spoon and again mash down with the end of the spoon until the mixture comes together. Taste and add more salt if necessary. Leave to simmer for 30 minutes to bring all the flavours together. At this stage you can leave it as a slightly chunky sauce or blend until smooth depending on your preference. Freeze any excess.

Loaf Cake, Maybe Lemon

This is just an excellent loaf cake, a great basis for adding a multitude of flavours or you can keep it simple with just a little lemon zest as in this recipe. It will keep well for a few days if wrapped well and stored in a tin.

240g soft, unsalted butter
180g caster sugar
3 free-range eggs
300g plain flour

1 teaspoon baking powder
1 teaspoon baking soda
juice and zest of 1 lemon

Preheat the oven to 170°C. Butter and line a 450g loaf tin.

In a bowl combine the flour, baking powder and baking soda. Stir with a whisk until there are no lumps. In a separate bowl cream the butter and sugar together until light and fluffy. Add the eggs one at a time with a tablespoon of the flour mixture for each egg, stirring well after each addition. Gently fold in the remaining flour mixture and finally add the lemon juice and zest, stirring until combined.

Pour into the loaf tin, sprinkling the top with another tablespoon or two of sugar if you would like a glossy, crunchy top. Bake for 1 hour until a skewer comes out clean.

Optional flavours to add to this cake:
This cake is like a blank canvas and can be the perfect base for many flavour additions.

Lemon Iced

Make the lemon cake as in the master recipe but ice with a simple icing made up of lemon juice and icing sugar. Combine 260g of sifted icing sugar with 110ml of lemon juice, then mix until you get a simple glaze. Pour over the cake while it's still warm (but not hot).

Raspberry or Any Berry

At the stage when you're putting the mixture in the tin, place half in the tin, sprinkle a handful of fresh raspberries or other seasonal berries such as blueberries or strawberries on top, then cover with the remaining mixture. Sprinkle with sugar and bake as above.

Orange Chocolate

Substitute 40g of the flour for cocoa, swap the lemon zest for orange zest and juice of half the orange and add 60g of chocolate chunks.

Soul Chicken Stock

My mother always had a pot of good chicken stock on the stove or in the fridge, and it's still a crime in my family to throw out a chicken carcass. Good stock is perfect convenience food, ready to add some noodles or veggies to turn into a delicious lunch. Bone broth is another food that's been having a moment recently but it's something people have been eating for centuries without any scientific research behind them, just the first-hand experience of its health benefits. I always make sure my chicken is organic, especially if I am boiling the bones afterwards. Yes, it is a little more expensive but in this case is well worth it. Stock is a great way to reduce your food waste – throughout the week save anything from vegetables you are prepping like carrot tops, coriander stalks or pea pods either in the fridge or freezer. Then after your Sunday roast simply add these to the chicken carcass along with the below ingredients.

1 chicken carcass

1 medium onion

2 stalks celery (with leaves intact)

2 carrots

6 stalks fresh flat-leaf or curly parsley

a sprig of thyme

1 teaspoon whole black peppercorns

any vegetable scraps from the week (see above)

3 litres cold water

Combine all the ingredients into a large pot and cover the water. Bring to the boil, reduce heat and simmer for 2½ to 3 hours.

Remove from the heat and using a potato masher, mash everything in the broth. This extracts all of the goodness and flavour. Strain through a fine sieve and let cool completely.

Store in the fridge for three days or freeze for up to 3 months.

Roast Leg of Lamb

When asked "what would your final meal be?" this is always my answer. It's one of my favourite things to eat and possibly the reason I am not a vegetarian. This lamb is marinated for 12 hours before you roast it, but if you don't have time for this step just slather the mixture on and pop straight in the oven. This is delicious with boiled new potatoes and a minted yoghurt, simply tear up some fresh mint leaves and add to natural yoghurt with a little water to loosen it out.

Serves 6–8

2 teaspoons cumin seeds
2 teaspoons coriander seeds
2 teaspoons mustard seeds
1 tablespoon black peppercorns
4 cloves of garlic, peeled
6 teaspoons sea salt
4 tablespoons olive oil
1 x 3–4 kg leg of lamb on the bone

Place all of the spices, garlic and olive oil into a pestle and mortar or blender and combine to a rough paste. Make a few small cuts in the flesh of the lamb and then smother with the mixture. Cover with tin foil and refrigerate for 12 hours.

Remove from the fridge and allow to come to room temperature two hours before you want to cook it. Heat the oven to 220°C.

Put the lamb in a roasting dish and cook on this high temperature for 30 minutes – this helps seal the outside and keep all the juices intact.

After half an hour reduce the temperature to 170°C and continue roasting for an hour to an hour and a half or until a meat thermometer in the thickest part of the leg reads 60°C. Remove from the oven, cover with foil and allow to rest in a warm place for 45 minutes before carving and devouring.

A SENSE OF HOME

Homemade Pizza that Is Actually Good

Pizza was one of those things that eluded me for a long time. I tried lots of methods and different dough bases, different sauces, more sauce, less sauce, baked fast on a high heat, baked slow on low, baked on a pizza stone (how many of those did I buy that cracked after the first use!). It wasn't until I came across this method from Josey Baker the San Franciscan baker that I felt I'd got it right. There are a couple of points to note:

You can bake this the same day you make it but you will get a much better result if you make the dough at least the day before but preferably up to 36 hours in advance. This dough needs time to relax and you will get a thinner and fluffier dough if you can plan ahead a little. Make sure your grill is on the highest setting, and keep an eye on it when it's under the grill! You will need a frying pan with a metal handle that can go under the grill.

Makes 4 pizzas

For the dough:
200ml lukewarm water
1 teaspoon sugar
1 packet (7g) instant yeast
400g white bread flour (if you don't have it you can substitute plain flour)
2 teaspoons sea salt
olive oil for cooking and drizzling on finished pizza

For the topping:
280g tomato sauce (see page 100)
or
600g cherry tomatoes, chopped

2 balls of fresh mozzarella
a handful of fresh basil or rocket (or both)

Add the sugar and the instant yeast to the lukewarm water, stir and leave for a few minutes. Put the bread flour into a large bowl, add the salt and mix with your (clean) hands.

Now pour the water and yeast mixture into the flour and using your hands bring the mixture together until you have a soft and wettish dough, with no lumps of flour. Cover with a clean tea towel and leave to rest for 30 minutes.

Turn the dough out onto a lightly floured surface and knead for about 5 minutes, then lightly oil the bowl and pop your dough back into it. Cover with cling film and place somewhere cool for between 12 and 36 hours.

A few hours before you want to bake the pizza, turn your dough out onto a lightly floured worktop and cut it into four equal portions. Shape each portion into a ball by pulling the edge of the dough into the centre, turning, pulling the next piece and so on until you get a round. Flip each ball over so the seam is on the bottom. Cover with a clean tea towel and leave to rest on your worktop for 2 to 3 hours.

When you are ready to bake your pizza, heat your grill to its highest setting. Place your pan on the hob also on a very high setting, put a teaspoon of olive oil in the pan and allow it to heat until it starts to smoke.

While the pan is heating, shape a ball of dough, stretch it out using your hands to press it and pull it to form a disk the size of your pan. Place the dough onto the pan and quickly spread with 70g of tomato sauce or 150g chopped cherry tomatoes. Rip up 80g of fresh mozzarella and toss evenly on top.

The pizza should be on the pan for 3 minutes so work quickly. After 3 minutes slide it under the grill for another 3 minutes until browned and sizzling. Remove from the heat, drizzle with a little extra virgin olive oil and sprinkle on some fresh basil or rocket if you like it.

Repeat with remaining dough balls.

Living Room

A place to relax, entertain,

unwind, connect.

W HAT DO YOU WANT your living room to be? It probably needs to be many things, a place to relax, entertain, unwind, connect. A place to nurture you. One of the first pieces of furniture you may buy will be the soul and anchor of your living room – your sofa. If there is not an immediately obvious position for it, try walking around the room with a small stool and sitting down in various locations. What do you want to look at from your sofa? Your television? A beautiful view from a window? An antique fireplace? Now, there are a couple of large furniture items in your home that are going to ask you to stretch the budget – your bed is one; your sofa is the other. If you think about how much time you spend on your sofa, it makes sense to buy the best you can afford. It should meet your requirements of comfort and size, and be beautiful too. This piece of furniture may need to double up as a guest bed, a spot for an afternoon nap, somewhere to squeeze onto with friends and family and a place to relax and unwind at the end of the day. A really well-made sofa will last you a lifetime, so choose wisely.

My Sofa Saga and Advice

Years ago when I was searching for a sofa for the house in Westmeath I came across a large tan leather vintage sofa in a furniture shop on Cow's Lane in Dublin. It was €2,000, which at that point in my life seemed a huge amount to pay. It had a patina that only aged leather can have, worn smooth and shiny on the corners with creases and crevices picking up light and adding such warmth and character. I couldn't justify buying it when things like cookers and dishwashers seemed like much more pressing purchases. Regretting the decision, I returned a few days later to find the sofa was gone. I chatted to the owner, explaining my regret. She showed me another couch that had come in – a two-seater costing €1,200. It was simple, with clean lines and upholstery of dark, moss-green tweed. Deciding to not let the chance slip by me again, I panicked and I bought it. However, when I got it home I realised that this little green tweed couch, clearly bought on a rebound, was just not going to work for me and my life. Four people in the house, two of them very rowdy and not very clean young boys … the thought of chocolate-smeared fingers trailing on to the beautiful green tweed was keeping me awake at night. Also you can always discount one

> It had a patina that only aged leather can have, worn smooth and shiny on the corners with creases and crevices.

seat from a sofa – a two-seater will seat two people but not for lounging in the evening watching a film, shovelling popcorn into your mouth and stretching your legs. The sofa was returned. The owner said she would call me if anything came in again like the tan leather one. A couple of months later I got the call and travelled again to Dublin. Indeed, there was a dark-brown leather three-seater. I borrowed the money and purchased it, and have never once regretted it. It has stood up to the two boys and the arrival of another one, to dogs, cats, spills and splutters and all the mess of daily life. It has certainly stood the test of time and has given me much joy.

Never buy a sofa that you haven't sat on. If you are purchasing online, then go to the showroom and sit on the sofa first. Something that looks smart on the screen can end up being hard and uncomfortable. Although many expensive

sofas come with the option of duck down cushions, I would recommend opting for a combination of down and foam – you need the foam for structure and the feathers for comfort. Also for a proper lounging sofa the seat should be a depth of 100cm, to allow maximum stretch and comfort for curling up.

If your current budget does not stretch to something custom-made (which is optimal) then opt for something with simple lines, a feature that makes a less expensive sofa look better. There really are such good and diverse options available now on the high street. You can add comfort by using feather cushions or buy a mini duvet made for a cot to use as a throw. The size of these is perfect and you can have a cover made from a favourite fabric. It will greatly add to the comfort of a hard seat pad and can be used as a decorative tool in the same way a large cushion would be.

Your Living Room Look

Look at your palette and see how you can incorporate this into your living room. If you are not at the point of doing a major overhaul then think about small ways you can add interest and colour. Not wanting to paint all of your walls? What about simply updating the trim and woodwork? You could probably complete this in two days and it will have an instant effect. Can you swap out some cushions? Update your lampshades? Add a new rug? Statement pieces like lamps, mirrors and vases can pick up on your accent colours and introduce drama and texture. Consider textures such as brushed metal, glossy porcelain or unglazed terracotta to add interest.

Lighting

Of course your living room will probably have an overhead light but I personally believe this should be your last resort for lighting the room and only used when vacuuming or decorating. Use a low wattage bulb (60w) here and have a dimmer switch fitted for more flexibility (see also page 25). Lamps are your friend here – lots of them. Lamps are a perfect opportunity to add a statement to your room. Think about scale – sometimes going larger than you think can make a bold statement and create interest and personality. Floor lamps are a great way to add drama. You want to create pools of interest and also areas where you have ample light to read, stitch on a button, file your nails, feed a baby.

At least two table lamps and one floor lamp should be enough for the average living room but as a general rule think of one source of light for every two to three seats in the room. There are so many great options available now in lighting and this is an area where you really don't have to spend a lot of money to get something great. Look for interesting bases, then you can add a more expensive lampshade or customise your shade by painting it. Any paper shade can be painted with a water-based paint. Seek out unique lampshades online. I particularly love pleated fabric-covered shades, they are having a moment currently thanks to British designers

like Ben Pentreath and Rita Konig. They're perfect for adding a bit of eccentricity (although they don't let out a huge amount of light). You can also cover a shade in paper. Buy some beautiful handmade paper, lay your lampshade over it and roll it along the paper, sketching out the pattern as you go. You will probably need two sheets of a standard-size wrapping paper to cover the shade.

If buying your shade separately, then as a general rule it should be ¾ the size of your lamp from base to fitting for table lamps and at least 45cm wide for floor lamps. Beware of buying a shade that is too small for a base; it never looks anything but cheap and skimpy. A great and empowering thing is to ask an electrician to fit the lamps to a socket controlled by one light switch so that you can illuminate all the lamps with one flick of a switch – such a joy!

As a last touch, look to your actual light switch plate – this is something that is often neglected but is the kind of detail that can really make a difference in a home. Spending a little extra on a beautiful brass switch, for instance, will immediately make your living room feel more luxe.

Wall Art

My rule for hanging wall art is to always hang the largest piece first and then add subsequent pieces from largest to smallest. You may make a few mistakes but your wall can easily be fixed with a daub of spackle and a touch of paint. Just follow your instinct. Beware of creating long alleyways between the pictures; if you see one, just knock the line off by adjusting a frame up or down, left or right to break it. If you don't have a large amount of art for your walls there are so many options around. Charity, antique or bric-a-brac shops are a great source for pictures, also check out end-of-year shows at art colleges. Children's art can be (indeed should be) framed and included in a living room display as can handmade papers, vintage photographs, letters or framed textiles – really the list is as endless as your imagination. Walls are your moment to show off a collection, if you have one, or any other items you admire or cherish. A length of wooden beads from India, a string of agate, a vintage brush, a beautifully weathered piece of driftwood and an embroidered textile that belonged to a grandmother have all found a place on a wall in my home. The interest, texture and whimsy added by such items will make your walls so much more individual.

Try choosing frames with different textures and finishes. Frames are also a great thing to look out for in charity shops and flea markets as people tend to only look at the picture and don't take notice that an awful artwork may be contained in a lovely frame.

Fresh, Clean, Fragrant

The air that you breathe in your living room should be as fresh and clean as possible. Having lots of plants will help with this and will also cleanse the air of pollutants, but remember to also open your windows once a week, letting the outside in to freshen the air. You can add natural scents, too, to help create the atmosphere you desire in this most important of rooms. Here are some of my favourite plants for the living room – I love them planted in simple terracotta pots, weathered by washing with some live yoghurt loosened with water and left outside for a few days to form a patina. Also look out for vintage terracotta pots at flea markets and charity shops.

- Scented geranium
- Pelargonium (geranium), especially with variegated leaves
- Rubber plant
- Ficus alii
- Spider plant
- Snake plant
- Succulents
- Chinese money plant
- Chinese evergreen

● ● ● ● ●

Homemade Potpourri

If the sound of potpourri makes you think of awful musty bowls of chemically dyed shavings and artificial flowers, then you need to think again. The word 'potpourri' comes from the French for rotted pot, not exactly enticing-sounding, but it comes from an age-old tradition of fermenting fragrant seeds, spices and flowers to create a beautiful aroma that can be enjoyed for years. Below are ideas of what to add to your potpourri.

Star anise	Allspice berries	Scented geranium leaves
Coffee beans	Fennel seeds	Citrus fruit peel
Cinnamon sticks	Bay leaves	Pine cones
Cloves	Eucalyptus leaves	Any fragrant flowers or herbs
Juniper berries	Rosemary twigs	

A Favourite Living Room Blend

100g any fragrant flower or herb combination

20g sea salt

100g spices of your choice (clove, cardamom, allspice)

20g brown sugar

10g orris root powder

1 tablespoon vodka

Lay out the flowers and herb leaves on a tray, sprinkle over the salt and leave for two days to dry. Now add all the other dry ingredients and sprinkle with the vodka, mixing everything together with your hands.

Place the mixture into an airtight container and leave to mature and develop its fragrance for a month. After a month scoop out as much as you want to use and place in a bowl of choice. Every time you want a refresh, just agitate the bowl for a fresh burst of scent. This fragrant mix should hold its scent for at least a year and possibly longer.

Touch and Texture in Your Living Room

Here is a place where you can really go all out with texture. Take a look at what you have then add in the opposite, creating texture is all about creating contrasts. Think of a deep sheepskin on a hardwood chair or a tweed cushion on a linen sofa.

If you have carpet on the floor why not lay a flat-weave rug on it? This is a great way to add your own stamp into rented accommodation, where you might be stuck with what is on the floor. If you have a wooden floor, then add a rug with texture like a Beni Ourain Moroccan rug. Personally I love the look of layered rugs. Making sure they have a common colour theme will make them harmonious rather than chaotic. You can mix different patterns and stripes this way and still have an overall look of harmony. Also flat-woven rugs can be used as table coverings – adding a console table behind a sofa is the perfect place to use a rug as a covering. Place a lamp, some books or a candle on top.

You can really get creative with texture in cushions – contrast them to your sofa for the most impact. For example, if your sofa is a flat, tightly woven fabric such as cotton or linen, you could add some cushions in warm fuzzy textures like tweed, sheepskin, wool, open-weave cotton and embroideries. Also think about adding vintage fabrics into the mix – beautifully printed vintage scarves can be made into cushions, perhaps you have one with a story attached to it stuffed away in a drawer? Or buy a small amount of a favourite fabric and have it made into a cushion, if you can't afford to upholster the whole sofa at least you can have this little personal piece.

The same rule goes for throws to add texture and warmth to your room. Think chunky knits and textured herringbones, knitted cotton, wool, silk or even cashmere: there is nothing quite like a cashmere throw to wrap around yourself when the evenings get chilly. It's like a massive cosy winter scarf to curl up in. Personally I don't really like mohair throws, they look great but somehow make my nose itch when I sit with one. But if you like them they are a great way to add another texture.

Don't forget the walls – a matt finish on the walls is very chic, just keep a little of the paint for touch-ups. When hung with pictures and frames the matt of the walls is a lovely contrast to the shine of glass or oil paint. A word of caution though – if you have small children with sticky fingers, a washable eggshell finish may be less stressful and more practical.

Sheepskin

A sheepskin in a home is a thing that feels very special to me – I cannot say enough good things about it. So, here is my ode to the sheepskin.

It's a versatile and cost-effective way of adding texture to your home. Throw one over the back of a chair, across the arm or back of the sofa, on top of a footstool, beside your bed for matchless luxury for your bare feet on rising.

Lay it in front of the fire for the dog or the cat to curl up on of a winter's evening. Use it as a cushion. If you have extra-deep windowsills throw one on to make an instant window seat. Pop it on garden furniture to add comfort (just remember to bring it in at night). Be like the Swedes and mount it on the wall.

Caring for Your Sheepskin

1. To wash, place it into a bath of cold water. Make sure you do not use hot as this will damage the fibres.
2. Add in a little mild shampoo. Agitate the sheepskin, paying attention to any grubby areas. Be gentle.
3. Rinse thoroughly. You may need to change the water several times and drain. You can finish it off by putting it in the washing machine on a spin cycle.
4. Air dry away from direct heat and sunlight.
5. Brush it with a wire dog brush. Job done!
6. In between washes keep your rug clean by brushing occasionally with a suitable brush (one designed for brushing pets works well).

Living Room Recipes

Living Room Eating

Sometimes you want a formal dinner party with all the bells and whistles; sometimes you just want a quiet supper in front of the TV. Many of us think that to entertain 'properly' we must supply the former but in many ways the latter is the greatest compliment of all – only your dearest friends, the ones we feel most comfortable around, would be invited for an informal supper.

Intimate Suppers for Four

Grab a fold-out table – just because it's a relaxed dinner doesn't mean you're eating takeout on your laps. Quite the contrary. Get out the linen and the best china (if you have it), place your table in front of the sofa with two chairs the other side. Light candles. Light the fire if it's chilly. For these meals you really want something that is easily served and hassle-free – what's the point if you spend the evening in the kitchen? So …

- Make the desserts a day or two ahead of time.
- Make the main courses the day before (they will actually be the better for it). Simply heat them in the oven before you serve.

I've given two seasonal living room suppers for you to choose from. All recipes are enough to serve four comfortably.

Spring/Summer Supper

- Lemon and Black Olive Chicken
- Green Quinoa
- Geranium-infused Citrus Sorbet

Autumn/Winter Supper

- Lamb Tagine
- Saffron Mashed Potato
- Olive Oil Chocolate Pots

Lemon and Black Olive Chicken

This dish has a Middle Eastern feel and the combination of sharp lemon and salty olives is delicious. It is really very simple to put together and can be assembled ahead of time (the night before would be good) and kept in the fridge then just thrown into a hot oven to cook when you are ready.

Serves 4

8 free-range chicken thighs
2 medium onions
1 lemon
2 pieces of preserved lemon, chopped (see page 286)
cloves from 1 head of garlic, peeled
24 kalamata black olives (pitted)
1 teaspoon sea salt
1 teaspoon whole coriander seeds, lightly crushed
1 teaspoon sumac
water
a bunch of fresh coriander, to serve

Pre heat the oven to 180°C.

Remove any excess fat from the chicken thighs and pat dry. Peel and slice the onions and slice the lemon, keeping the slices as thin as you can. Place into the bottom of a roasting pan and evenly scatter over the cloves of garlic, olives and chopped preserved lemon.

Lay the chicken thighs on top and sprinkle with the salt, coriander seeds and sumac. At this point you can place in the fridge until you are ready to cook, or proceed as follows. Add enough cold water to cover the onions and lemons and roast in the oven for 45 minutes. Meanwhile roughly chop the coriander.

Remove the pan from the oven, check that the chicken is cooked through and scatter with the chopped coriander.

Green Quinoa

I like to serve this quinoa with the lemon chicken. Somewhere between a salad and side of grains, it is light and fresh. It doesn't take long to bring together and is best made immediately before serving to keep all the ingredients fresh. To save time, however, you can cook the quinoa the night before.

200g (uncooked weight) quinoa
3 tablespoons olive oil
40g fresh flat leaf parsley
40g fresh coriander
10g fresh mint
10g fresh lemon verbena (optional)
juice from ½ a lemon
a pinch of sea salt

Rinse the quinoa and cook in a pot of boiling water for 15 minutes or until cooked through – it will be soft with the grains beginning to sprout. Drain, place in a bowl and add the olive oil. Chop the fresh herbs finely and add to the bowl along with the lemon juice and salt. Stir and serve.

Geranium-infused Citrus Sorbet

Sharp and clean but with a slight floral undertone, this is like a grown-up orange sherbet. I have infused the orange syrup with the leaves of a scented geranium, one of my favourite plants and scents. You could substitute thyme or lemon verbena leaves for the geranium, or leave it out altogether. This can be made days, or even weeks, in advance.

Serves 4

zest and juice of 1 orange (or 2 clementines)
juice of 3 lemons and zest of 1
140g caster sugar
150ml water
3–4 scented geranium leaves, picked

Place the orange and lemon juice and zest, sugar, water and geranium leaves into a pan and bring to a simmer for 5 minutes or until all the sugar is dissolved. Allow to cool, then transfer to a metal bowl and place in the freezer for 2 hours.

Remove from the freezer and check – you should have a semi-frozen sorbet with most of the outside frozen and the centre still a little soft. If it is not ready put it back in the freezer for another while.

When it is ready remove from the freezer and empty into a food processor. Blend until smooth, then scrape into an airtight container with a lid. Freeze until ready to serve. Delicious served with some dark chocolate grated over the top.

Lamb Tagine

Making this lamb tagine ahead really enhances and matures the flavour. You will need a cast-iron lidded pot for this, something that can go on top of the cooker and into the oven too. I have added dried limes which bring a beautiful depth of flavour to this tagine, they are available in any Middle-eastern food shop or online. You could add a squeeze of fresh lime juice at the end but it won't be quite the same.

Serves 4 with leftovers

700g diced lamb shoulder
2 teaspoons coriander seeds
2 teaspoons cumin seeds
1 teaspoon ground cinnamon
1 teaspoon chilli flakes
2 tablespoons sweet paprika
2 medium onions
3 cloves of garlic
2 tablespoons olive oil
2 x 400g tins of whole tomatoes
800ml vegetable stock
300g whole dried apricots
1 teaspoon saffron threads
3 dried limes (optional)
fresh coriander and mint, to serve

Put the lamb pieces into a bowl. Bash the coriander and cumin seeds in a pestle and mortar. Sprinkle these, along with the cinnamon, chilli and paprika, over the lamb and rub it well into the meat. Peel and chop the onions; peel and crush the garlic.

Pour 1 tablespoon of the oil into your casserole pot and place on a medium to high heat. When the oil is hot, drop the meat into the pan in

batches, just cooking as much as will cover the bottom of the pan at any one time. Brown the meat on all sides and set aside on a plate nearby. Once all the meat is browned and removed, add the chopped onions to the pot with the other tablespoon of oil. Scrape any bits from the bottom of the pan, stirring until the onions are nicely softened.

Now put the meat back into the pot along with the tins of tomatoes, stock, garlic, apricots, saffron threads and dried limes (if using). Preheat your oven to 180°C.

Simmer, stirring occasionally for about 40 minutes, then transfer into the oven with the lid on. Cook for 2 to 3 hours, checking it after 2 hours. If it is still very watery you can remove the lid for the final half hour to thicken the sauce. Keep an eye on it though so it doesn't dry out.

If making in advance, allow to cool completely then refrigerate until the following day. Reheat gently over a medium heat.

Remove the dried limes before serving but squeeze out their juice first with the back of a spoon.

Saffron Mashed Potato

This golden mashed potato is homely and decadent at the same time. I first came across the idea of saffron mashed potato in a book called *Relish* by Joanna Weinberg. Joanna adds an egg white in her recipe, I prefer not to and add a little more milk to make them looser but adjust to your own taste. Add the milk to the mash while it is at boiling point to help make it really light and fluffy.

Serves 4

500g potatoes
75ml–100ml milk
1 teaspoon saffron threads
30g butter
a pinch of sea salt

Peel the potatoes and cut in half. Boil in a medium-size pot until done, then drain and mash.

In a small saucepan heat the milk with the saffron strands until it begins to boil, then add immediately to the hot mashed potato, along with the butter.

Continue mashing until you have a creamy consistency with no lumps, then taste and season with a little sea salt.

A personal note to finish – I find mashed potato greatly benefits from a stint in the oven. If you want to give it a try, pile it into an ovenproof dish, dot some butter on the top, cover with foil and slide into the oven at 180°C for half an hour. This gives you the perfect opportunity to fix your hair before the guests arrive.

Olive Oil Chocolate Pots

These are a decidedly grown-up version of a chocolate mousse. The addition of olive oil not only adds a lovely flavour but also combines with the eggs and chocolate to make a delicious silky texture. Make sure you use a very light olive oil, otherwise the flavour can be too intense. A little extra virgin olive oil drizzled on at the end will add a spiced peppery kick. I like to weigh the olive oil here instead of measuring by volume as the quantities are quite small and it is more accurate. These can be made the day before and kept in the fridge until ready to serve.

Serves 4

80g dark chocolate (60–70%)
20g caster sugar
2 large free-range eggs, separated
30g light olive oil
a drizzle of extra virgin olive oil, to serve

Preheat the oven to 140°C.

Separate your eggs and set aside. Place the chocolate and olive oil in a medium-size pan over a very low heat. Stir until the chocolate is melting, remove from the heat while there are still some lumps of chocolate and continue to stir. The residual heat will melt the remaining chocolate and this way you avoid burning or overcooking it. Allow the chocolate mixture to cool while you get on with the rest. Spread the sugar onto a baking sheet lined with parchment paper and place in the oven for 10 minutes to warm.

In a clean metal bowl whisk the egg whites until they form soft peaks. Remove the sugar from the oven and slowly add it a tablespoon at a time to the whites, whisking constantly.

Add the egg yolks to the cooled chocolate mixture and stir until thick, I find a rubber spatula best for this.

Add a third of the glossy egg whites to the chocolate mixture and stir

well. Now add the remaining egg white and fold into the mixture very gently with a large metal spoon, you don't want to knock out the air so be careful. Scoop into four ramekins or small glasses and chill for at least 3 hours until set. Serve with a drizzle of extra virgin olive oil over each pot.

Movie Night In

Another lovely informal evening to host in your living room is a movie night in. I would say six to ten people is a good number. You won't be serving dinner at this; drinks and snacks will suffice. This is a list of some of my favourite films, most of them classics and all of them worth repeated watching. Work backwards from the time you want the movie to end and invite people to arrive half an hour before with a strict policy of show time … if you're late you miss the beginning of the movie! Movie start times listed below are for an approximate 11.30 pm finish.

Dances With Wolves	8.30 pm
The English Patient	8.45 pm
Out of Africa	8.50 pm
Cold Mountain	9.00 pm
Atonement	9.30 pm
The Assassination of Jesse James	8.50 pm
A Single Man	9.50 pm
All About Eve	9.10 pm
The African Queen	9.45 pm
Fight Club	9.10 pm
The Shawshank Redemption	9.10 pm
Dangerous Liaisons	9.30 pm
Sophie's Choice	9.00 pm
The Deer Hunter	8.30 pm
The Age of Innocence	9.10 pm

Kind Hearts and Coronets	9.45 pm
In the Mood for Love	9.50 pm
Double Indemnity	9.50 pm
Gone With the Wind	7.30 pm
Gosford Park	9.20 pm
The King's Speech	9.30 pm
Pan's Labyrinth	9.30 pm
The Piano	9.30 pm
The Portrait of a Lady	9.00 pm
The Remains of the Day	9.15 pm
The Talented Mr Ripley	9.10 pm
Whatever Happened to Baby Jane?	9.15 pm

Movie snacks

All the recipes given below should be enough to sustain your movie gang comfortably throughout the viewing.

- Coconut, Dark Chocolate and Sea-salted Popcorn
- Sweet Potato and Potato Herbed Salt Crisps
- A Cheese Table
- Red Onion Marmalade
- Lime Coriander Chicken Wings
- Fruit Crumble Crisp With Minted Cream

Coconut, Dark Chocolate and Sea-salted Popcorn

Everyone loves popcorn, don't they? This recipe is a highly addictive combination of sweet and salty. Coconut flakes add texture; if you can't buy them toasted then toast your own on a baking tray for 5 to 10 minutes in a medium oven.

200g dark chocolate (60–70%)
200g popcorn
200g toasted coconut flakes
a sprinkle of sea salt (unless you are using pre-salted microwave popcorn)

Grate one bar of chocolate and chop the other into small lumps about the size of your little fingernail. This means that some of the chocolate (grated) will melt very quickly and the chunks will remain, but they will soften and clump with the popcorn and coconut flakes. Tip all the chocolate into a large bowl.

Pop the popcorn using your preferred method (on the hob or in the microwave). When completely popped and while it is still hot, pour the popcorn onto the chocolate and stir with a spoon. Scatter the coconut and salt (if using) on top and stir once or twice. Eat straight away while still warm.

Sweet Potato and Potato Herbed Salt Crisps

Homemade crisps – why bother? Well, make these beauties and your question will be answered. I recommend making a large bowl of these then serving them to your guests in individual bowls, otherwise a fight may break out. The potatoes will need to be soaked for at least half an hour in cold water to remove the starch, but you can do this the night before, making sure they are completely submerged in the water. The herbed salt can also be prepared the night before, so all you have to do is cook them before everyone arrives. They really are best eaten straight away, but this won't be a problem as there will not be any leftovers.

2 floury potatoes, scrubbed (Russet, Rooster or Maris Piper would all work well)

2 medium sweet potatoes, scrubbed

2 teaspoons sea salt

1 sprig of fresh rosemary

1 sprig of fresh thyme

1 teaspoon aromatic seeds (caraway, fennel or coriander all work well)

½–1 teaspoon black pepper

100–200ml sunflower oil for frying

Slice your potatoes as thinly as you can, using a mandolin or a very sharp knife. Leave to soak in ice-cold water for at least half an hour to remove some of the starch.

Now prepare your salt. Chop the herbs very finely and put in a small bowl along with the salt and seeds. Mix everything together.

Slice the sweet potatoes as thinly as you can and set aside. (They don't need to be soaked.)

Place your oil in a heavy pot with deep sides, you need at least 4 to 6cm of oil. Heat the oil until it's very hot – test it by dropping a piece of potato in – if it sizzles and bubbles it's ready for frying. Drain and dry your white potatoes and place them with the sweet potatoes.

Fry the potatoes in batches, being careful not to crowd the pot. When golden, lift them out with a slotted spoon and place on kitchen paper to drain. When all the potatoes and sweet potatoes are cooked transfer to a large bowl, sprinkle over the herbed salt and black pepper and toss to coat. Serve immediately in individual bowls.

A Cheese Table

A cheese board is truly a wondrous thing and takes little or no time to prepare. Set out china plates, napkins and knives on your coffee table (or a folding table). Plan on buying 100g–150g of cheese per person. Usually four to five different cheeses make a good board, but be aware that it's better to have a decent piece of each and a smaller selection than teeny bits of lots of different cheeses. There are five main types of cheese to choose from: fresh, soft, semi-soft, hard and blue. Ideally select one from each category to give your board a nice variety of texture and flavour.

1. **A fresh cheese** is mild and creamy with a soft consistency. It is not aged and is eaten very soon after it is made so the flavour is clean and light. Example: chèvre.
2. **A soft cheese** has an edible rind with a mild flavour but stronger than a fresh cheese. The longer these cheeses are aged, the runnier they will be and the sharper the flavour of the rind. Examples: Brie, Camembert, Délice de Bourgogne.
3. **A semi-soft cheese** is mellow, buttery and nutty. Examples: Mossfield, Comté.
4. **A hard cheese** is dry and sharper in flavour. Examples: Cheddar, Manchego.
5. **A blue cheese** has had a specific mould introduced into it to sharpen the flavour. Ranging from mild to sharp, you can find blue cheese in soft and semi-soft forms. Examples: Gorgonzola, Stilton.

There are other cheeses that may be delicious but for me, have no place on a cheese board. These include feta, ricotta, any cheese with a fruit or seed added to it, any smoked cheese, Parmesan or Mozzarella. They all have their place to shine but the cheese board is not it.

Make sure you serve cheese at room temperature. Take it out of the fridge at least an hour before you want to serve, unwrap it and set it down on the board. Give each cheese a bit of breathing space on the board, making sure no cheese is touching another. Set each cheese with its own cutting knife so that there is no cross-contamination when people are selecting. Cover the board with a damp tea towel until just before you are serving. Here are some suggestions for a perfect combination.

An Irish Selection

We are lucky to have the most wonderful dairy in Ireland and subsequently the most wonderful cheese, with the variety growing every year.

- Mossfield
- Cashel Blue
- Strong Irish Cheddar
- Ardsallagh goat's cheese

An International Selection

This array of cheese from Spain, Italy and France includes some of my favourites.

- Manchego
- Gorgonzola
- Délice de Bourgogne
- Comté

Along with the cheeses, set out bowls of something crunchy like walnuts or smoked almonds and some fresh fruit. Depending on the season, you could have a bowl of clementines, figs, perfectly ripe pears, grapes or apricots. Offer a variety of crackers, oatcakes, water biscuits, something salty. Beware of overly herbed or flavoured crackers, good cheese needs a vehicle, not something to overpower the flavour. A variety of chutneys is also good to have: try this red onion marmalade as one of them.

Red Onion Marmalade

3 red onions
4 tablespoons olive oil
100g brown sugar
2 bay leaves
50ml balsamic vinegar
100ml red wine

Makes about 2 jars of marmalade

Peel the onions and slice them into thin rounds. Put the oil into a deep frying pan over a low to medium heat and add the onion slices and the bay leaves. Cook slowly for about 30 minutes until the onions are dark and beginning to caramelise.

Add the sugar, vinegar and red wine and simmer for another 30 minutes until the mixture is glossy and thick. Allow to cool.

Spoon into sterilised jars (see page 242) and store in a cool place for up to six months. You can eat it straight away but it will taste better after a few weeks.

Lime Coriander Chicken Wings

Chicken wings are a perfect movie snack. Remember to give people a napkin to wipe their hands and to have an empty bowl for bones.

1 tablespoon sea salt
1 teaspoon black pepper
2 cloves of garlic (finely chopped)
1 teaspoon paprika
60g butter (very soft)
juice and zest of 1 lime
1 tablespoon honey
a bunch of fresh coriander
1 kg chicken wings

Preheat the oven to 180°C.

Place the salt, pepper, garlic, paprika, butter, lime zest and juice and honey into a large bowl and stir well, making sure no lumps are left. Coarsely chop half of the bunch of coriander (including the stalks) and add to the mixture.

Throw in the chicken wings and massage with your hands so that every wing is well coated. Empty the wings onto a baking tray lined with parchment and roast in the oven for 30 to 40 minutes until the wings are cooked and crispy. Remove from the oven and sprinkle on the remaining fresh coriander. Eat immediately – you will need finger bowls and napkins!

Fruit Crumble Crisp with Minted Cream

Crumble may seem like a strange thing to serve at a movie night. The reason I chose it is because once on a yoga retreat after a long day of sweating and bending the evening was planned to watch inspiring *TED Talks* on a large screen. As we snuggled up on the sofa, exhausted from our physical efforts, Minnie (the host) walked in with a tray of crumble and custard. There was something so nostalgic, comforting and decadent about being handed a bowl of crunchy fruit crumble with steaming custard while enjoying a fabulous show. I never forgot it. This recipe is made using melted butter so the topping has a slightly different texture than a traditional crumble. I have used plums and blackberries here but really you could use any fruit such as apples, apricots or blueberries. A couple of sprigs of mint added to the fruit are barely detectable but add that slight note of flavour. If your fruit is very sweet, you may not need the honey: adjust accordingly. I like to serve it with a cream that has been infused with mint leaves. Make sure you use a good mint such as apple or chocolate mint – do not use spearmint, it is too strong and overpowering here.

For the filling:
600g plums
100g blackberries
1 tablespoon honey
1 tablespoon chopped fresh mint

For the crumble crisp topping:
160g butter
220g plain flour
60g sugar
80g light brown sugar
1 teaspoon cinnamon
120g whole almonds, chopped (I like to chop them lengthways)

For the minted cream:

227g double cream

2–3 good sprigs of fresh mint

Preheat the oven to 180°C.

First infuse your cream. Bash the mint up a bit to release the oils then add the sprigs directly into the cream container and allow to infuse for 24 hours.

Halve the plums and remove the stones. Place in an ovenproof dish and drizzle over the honey, then throw in the blackberries and fresh mint.

To make the crumble crisp, melt your butter in a pan on a low heat. Measure the flour, sugars, cinnamon and chopped almonds into a bowl and stir, then pour over the melted butter and combine.

Sprinkle the crumble mixture over the fruit and bake in the oven for 35 to 40 minutes until golden and crispy on the top.

While it is baking whip your cream (removing the mint first). Serve warm with the freshly whipped minted cream.

A Tea Tray for One

After Obi, my eldest son, was born we moved from Manhattan to Brooklyn. We may as well have moved to Outer Mongolia. Brooklyn in those days wasn't what it is today and our friends' faces dropped when we informed them. Back then moving to Brooklyn was seen as giving up – it was a badge of honour to continue the fight against the gentrification and rising rents in Manhattan. But with a small baby in a tiny East Village studio apartment above a 24-hour kebab shop, the badge of honour was wearing thin, common sense was kicking in and I wanted more space and if possible proximity to some sort of green space.

This was a lonely time. Being the first of my New York friends to have a child meant that most of them were still out partying, and very few of them ventured to Brooklyn … ever. My partner Mark was working nights, and holed up in my Brooklyn apartment I began a ritual of setting myself a tea tray every night after he left. On it went my favourite bone china cup and saucer, a silver spoon, a little plate with a biscuit or small treat and a cloth napkin. It became a ritual, a moment of self-nourishment, that helped me through that time – I guess now you would call it mindfulness.

The Japanese give great weight to the ceremony of drinking tea – it is considered a spiritual experience, a meditation, with each part of the process given space and reverence. Taking the time to appreciate the small things in life, such as tea drinking, is something we all need to do more of.

The Perfect Cup of Tea

In Ireland we have an obsession with tea. It is the first thing someone will offer you when you arrive at their house, a customary welcome. God forbid you don't get offered a cup – wars have been started for less. I had a friend who didn't drink tea for years. I never knew what to do with her when she came to visit. After an awkward exchange, I would sit with my mug of tea and she with a glass of water but it never felt right. She has since taken it up as she said not drinking it became far too stressful in social situations.

So ... do you need to learn to make tea? Not really. But sometimes I want more than the bag in the cup, a bit of pomp and ceremony. Perhaps something more refined, a Lapsang Souchong, an Earl Grey or an Oolong. So get yourself:

- A teapot
- The finest china (cup and saucer, thank you)
- Tea leaves of choice
- A tea strainer
- A silver teaspoon

Take the time to set a tray for yourself. Leave the TV off; don't even read a book, just drink the tea and maybe eat a slice of cake or one of your favourite biscuits. Enjoy every mouthful and every part of the act. Listen to the sound of the tea pouring into the china cup, the spoon against the saucer. This is the essence of a tea tray for one.

Honey Sesame Plum Cake

This is the perfect cake for a cup of tea – moist and sweet, but not too sweet. The combination of plum and sesame seeds is inspired by the east but the cake is very much a western creation. It will keep for several days and possibly, some would say, even improves after a day or two. I strongly recommend grinding your own almonds for this recipe as it really affects the texture of the cake but pre-ground almonds will also work. I like to bake it in a fluted long tart tin because it looks terribly pretty but you could also bake it in a round 20cm tin.

Makes approx. 8 slices

140g caster sugar
90g unsalted butter (at room temperature)
30g plain flour
2 free-range eggs
140g almonds (preferably freshly ground)
zest of a small orange
3 tablespoons sesame seeds
1 plum, halved and pitted then sliced into 4 rounds
13 whole almonds to decorate

For the honey syrup:
juice from the above orange
2 tablespoons honey

Preheat the oven to 180°C. Grease a 10 x 35cm tart tin and line the bottom with baking parchment.

Cream the butter and sugar in a large bowl. Add 1 egg, sprinkle in half the flour and combine. Add the other egg with the remaining flour and mix (don't worry if the mixture curdles a bit).

Stir in the ground almonds and orange zest, then empty the mixture into

the tin and smooth the top. Sprinkle sesame seeds on the top completely covering the surface, then place the sliced plum at equal intervals along the cake dotting the whole almonds around each slice. Bake for 30 to 35 minutes or until a cake skewer comes out clean.

To make the syrup, put the orange juice and honey into a small pan and simmer for 10 to 15 minutes on a medium heat until the mixture has halved in quantity and become think and syrupy. When the cake is ready, remove from the oven and brush the warm syrup all over the warm cake.

Bedroom

Your bedroom should be
a cocoon, a sanctuary.

O F ALL THE ROOMS IN YOUR HOUSE, your bedroom should be a cocoon, a sanctuary and a place where you can get good-quality sleep. We spend a third of our lives in bed and it is the last room you see every night and the first thing you look at every morning, so it makes sense to put some time and effort into getting it to look and feel exactly the way you want. Creating a calming environment is really important and easy to achieve by following a few simple guidelines.

Your bed should be comfortable. You should be getting seven to nine hours of sleep in it every night, so buy the best you can afford – this is one area where you shouldn't cut corners. There are different types of mattresses available – which one you choose will depend on your needs. A good mattress should support your body in a neutral position without applying too much pressure at any one point. There is medical research that confirms a firmer mattress is preferable and better for your back.

Now to the nuts and bolts of the bed, starting with the foundations, or bases that go under the mattresses. A box spring is a type of base that contains a series of metal coils, and has the benefits of absorbing shock, raising the height of your bed (for ease of entrance and exit) and extending the life of your mattress. You can also have a foundation with a more solid structure, such as solid or slatted wood, usually with a cover.

On top of these go your mattress. Foam or memory foam mattresses, popular in recent years, can be a good option if you sleep with a partner

who tosses and turns a lot as they are less bouncy and so less disturbing. However, I am not a big fan – I find your body temperature rises with these and sleeping can become a hot and sweaty affair. To counteract the problem of overheating, companies have come up with a gel option that incorporates the qualities of memory foam but also a gel that acts to balance out the temperature. I personally favour a pocket-sprung mattress, where springs are sealed into fabric pockets and sewn together. These won't make you warmer in the night and won't dip in the middle either.

What goes on top of your mattress (a mattress topper) is also a matter of personal taste. If budget allows, I recommend a feather-filled one as a luxurious addition to your bed. Most good homeware departments will stock these and they can make a firm mattress feel cushy and enveloping while still providing the support you need.

A SENSE OF HOME

So, a good recipe for the perfect bed is a firm pocket spring mattress topped with a feather-filled mattress topper. Have two square large pillows at the back, two feather pillows in front of these and one or two square or oblong smaller feather cushions in front of those. This arrangement will make sitting up in bed to read so comfortable, and you can throw some excess pillows on the floor when you're settling down to sleep. All bed linen should be made from natural fibres like cotton or linen, because not only do they look great, they are more breathable than synthetic fibres, which is important for the regulation of temperature at night.

Storage

Store your items so you can see what you have and easily access it without rummaging. Try the Marie Kondo method of folding items in a vertical row, so everything is visible when you open your drawers (ingenious idea) or stack clothing (Benetton shop style) on shelves in your wardrobe; just make sure everything is visible. I like to keep items stored in baskets and folded vertically so when I pull out a basket every item can be seen. On the basket note, believe me when I say you can never have enough baskets in a house – they are true work horses, being useful, beautiful and natural. Keeping clothes clean and stored properly will mean that you are much more likely to wear the clothes you have. Wardrobes should smell nice and contain natural repellents for moths – avoid chemical mothballs: they may kill moths but are bad news for humans and pets (see pomanders, page 175).

The Balance of Light and Dark

Both light *and* darkness are vital to get right in a bedroom. Darkness prompts the body to create melatonin and thus aid a good night's sleep, something we all need. If you live in an urban environment, street lights can make your room too bright, making it difficult to get to sleep, and wherever you live, summer's early sunrise can cause you to wake earlier than you'd like to. Your room should be like a bat cave at night – really good blackout blinds are freely available and will cut out any external light source. Hang curtains too, both for their aesthetic effect and also as an additional light and noise barrier. At the very least, sleep with an eye mask on. I struggled with wearing one at night for years, but too many early summer morning awakenings and bad curtains while travelling meant that I found it became a necessity, and simply trained myself to use it … now I can't sleep without one. There are many different kinds on the market, some have lavender in them so have the added benefit of aromatherapy as well as blocking out the light. I would recommend making sure your eye mask has an adjustable strap – it is surprising how variable head size is and a 'one size fits all' approach is not the best here. It needs to be tight enough to stay on your head but not so tight you wake up with a headache.

Aim to have several levels of lighting in your bedroom. Keep bedside lights simple – they only need to create a pool of light that allows you to read. An overhead light (preferably on a dimmer to give flexibility) should illuminate the whole room so you can get dressed easily. If you put make-up on in your bedroom, you will need adequate lighting for that. Side lighting is preferable for a dressing table or mirror. One wall lamp either side of a wall mirror is ideal, set the light so that the bulb is at eye level. Bulb type is important – a warm white 75 to 100W bulb is perfect and more flattering.

Bedroom Colours

This is not the room in which to experiment with bright colours: you want an environment containing soft, soothing tones that will help you relax and unwind. Blue is a good bedroom colour as it is said to lower blood pressure and reduce your heart rate; I also love pale pinks and blush colours for a bedroom. You can stop these from looking too feminine by staying away from frills and flounces. Dark walls can also be very comforting in a bedroom, having an enveloping, womblike effect.

Instead of sticking to one colour, creating a tonal palette will help to induce a calm atmosphere while still feeling interesting and avoiding being bland. To do this, pick your wall colour then build out from that, adding darker and lighter shades in the same tone for the trim, floor covering and accents such as lampshades and rugs. Think about texture too, painting walls in a matt finish and your trim in high gloss is very effective, either in the same colour or slightly darker or lighter shades. Add in some neutrals for a harmonious feel. If, when everything is in place, you think the bedroom needs a hint of something to spice it up, put a contrasting coloured or patterned throw on your bed or a dramatic piece of art on the wall.

Pure and Fragrant Bedroom Air

We all have some level of stress in our lives so a good night's sleep is essential. Of course there are times in our lives that are more stressful than others and it is at these times, when we need it most, that sleep can often evade us. The air in your bedroom should be fresh, pure, clean and calming. Pure air will help you sleep more soundly. The most straightforward and natural way to purify your air is to introduce some key plants to the bedroom (see below for examples). Some plants also have the added benefit of a sleep-inducing scent. Place your air-purifying plants in pretty pots and pop them next to your bed or on your windowsill.

Look into, also, getting a salt lamp for your room – these lamps, made of Himalayan salt crystals, have multiple benefits and help to keep your air clean and free from dust, pollen and other impurities.

Air Purifying and Scented Plants

Lavender

Most of us know the calming and soothing properties of lavender oil, so it makes sense that a growing lavender plant beside your bed will do the same. Pinch a leaf and rub it between your hands briskly, then cup your hands over your face and take ten slow breaths in and out of your nose.

Lemon Verbena and Lemon Balm

The lemony smell released by both the above plants is another favourite of mine and is also linked to calming the central nervous system. Apply the same ritual as above with one of their leaves to calm you just before bed.

Aloe Vera

Apart from being very easy to maintain (they don't need much watering), aloe vera plants are great at purifying the air. They release oxygen at night, helping you to get a restful night's sleep.

Snake Plant

As with the aloe vera above, the snake plant (also called Mother in Law's Tongue because of the sharp leaves!) releases oxygen at night and helps to purify the air. It's incredibly hardy and is also a good choice if your bedroom doesn't get much natural light as it can tolerate a low-light environment.

English Ivy

It is said that an English ivy plant can help eliminate the symptoms of allergies and asthma. Place one in your bedroom – it will purify the air, ridding it of mould and toxins.

Pillow Spray

I recently discovered pillow spray, and now I swear by it. This little bottle of scented water can live on your bedside table to be sprayed onto your pillow before retiring for calming, sleep-promoting scents.

Lavender	Neroli	Sandalwood
Ylang ylang	Geranium	Clary sage
Bergamot	Frankincense	Marjoram
Chamomile	Vetiver	Cedarwood

Some of my favourite combinations are:
- Bergamot 15 drops, geranium 10 drops, vetiver 5 drops, neroli 5 drops
- Lavender 10 drops, geranium 10 drops, marjoram 5–8 drops, clary sage 5 drops
- Frankincense 10 drops, vetiver 10 drops, chamomile 10 drops, cedarwood 5 drops

Pillow Spray Recipe

6ml vodka

170ml distilled water (available in pharmacies)

essential oil combination (30–35 drops of essential oil in total)

You'll need a 200ml glass jar with a spray attachment.

Combine your selection of essential oils in a ceramic dish. Pour into the spray bottle, add the vodka and water and shake well.

Experiment with different scents to come up with your favourite. This spray will keep indefinitely as the alcohol acts as a preservative. Also these sprays make really lovely personal gifts.

• • • • •

An Aromatic Cleanse for Winter Woes

This blend of oils originates in medieval times and is said to have been worn by thieves who stole from the poor during the plague and used this blend to keep them healthy. Well, I can't say it will stave off the bubonic plague but certainly it will help your sinuses and contains antibacterial and antifungal properties.

7 drops lemon oil

3 drops eucalyptus oil

2 drops rosemary oil

8 drops clove oil

4 drops cinnamon oil

Combine the oils into a small ceramic jar. Add several drops to a diffuser or a bowl of 100ml of hot water and place near your bed.

Alternatively add a couple of drops to 2 tablespoons of a carrier oil of your choice, such as olive oil or coconut oil. Rub onto the soles of your feet, put on warm socks, and take yourself to bed.

Clothing Care and Scent

Keep your clothes smelling fresh and moth-free by keeping these little bags in your wardrobe. You can also add conkers if you have any, they have no scent but are great moth repellents. You can either buy or make your own cloth bags – little organza jewellery pouches are ideal and inexpensive.

Pomanders

I've always loved these studded citrus fruits, but never knew that they were good for repelling pesky little winged clothes-munchers: cloves are one of the most effective moth repellents. The fruit is studded with cloves and then rolled in spices and orris root, a powder derived from the root of the iris flower which acts as a scent fixative and will help to greatly prolong the scent of your pomander. You can easily buy it online.

2 x firm, tight-skinned pieces of citrus fruit
a jar of cloves
1 tablespoon each of:

ground ginger   cinnamon
allspice   orris root
nutmeg

Stud the fruit all over with the cloves, leaving space to tie a ribbon on if you want to hang it. Mix the spices together on a large plate and roll your fruit in it until it's completely covered. Leave to cure for three weeks.

The fruit will dry out and shrink. When ready, you can tie a ribbon around it and hang it in your wardrobe or place in a drawer to keep precious jumpers moth-free.

Wardrobe Sachets

100g dried lavender

20g cloves

20g crushed cinnamon stick (approx. 4–6 depending on size)

Simply fill the bag with the mixture, tie it closed and hang it in your wardrobe. Replace every six months or when it has lost its scent. Note: some of the scent may linger on your clothing.

This will make 6 small or 2 large bags.

The Feel of Comfort

Texture is key in a bedroom – surround yourself with materials such as cashmere, sheepskins, linens and cotton to give warmth and comfort. A cashmere wrap draped along the bottom of your bed can be swiftly drawn up around your shoulders if you are sitting up in bed reading. The modern-day bed jacket!

Pay attention also to the feel of the flooring in your bedroom: apart from the bathroom, this is the one area where you are likely to be walking around in your bare feet. For this reason, I am fond of a carpet in a bedroom. Yes, I love wood but in your bedroom carpet just feels luxurious. If you have wooden floors then lay down big rugs and think about the feel of them – tufted wool, or silk if you can afford it, is perfect here. A small sheepskin rug on the floor where your feet touch the ground on rising will be a welcome warm hug for your toes every morning.

The most important thing you will touch in your bedroom are your sheets. Think about how long you spend between them … many of us balk at the price of a good set of sheets but then splurge five times that on a bag that we might only use a couple of times a year. So buy the best sheets you can possibly afford – it's the simplest thing you can do to upgrade your sleep. Once you sleep in good sheets it is impossible to go back. Let's

go through the nuts and bolts of sheet types – there are many options out there and it can be a bit overwhelming, but you just need to know a few simple pointers.

Thread Count

This term 'thread count' refers to the number of threads per square inch in the fabric. There are sheets on the market that have up to 1,000, but the reality is that this is unnecessary. What type of cotton thread is being used is just as important. A better cotton thread in a lower thread count will be a softer sheet. The magic number really is somewhere between 240 and 400; after that you are wasting your money.

Fabric

For really good sheets your number one choice should be certified Egyptian cotton. This cotton grows with a longer fibre and so makes for a superior and softer sheet. After Egyptian is Pima, sometimes labelled *Supima*, which is a trademark. This is also very good quality with a long cotton fibre. If it is not Egyptian or Pima, then the quality will be inferior as it is regular cotton which has a shorter fibre so the tiny threads poke out, creating a sheet that will not be as smooth.

Weave

The next choice is the weave, or the way the fabric is woven. The warp (vertical threads on the loom) and weft (horizontal treads which are woven through) can be manipulated in different ways to give varying textures. Percale is a plain-weave cotton, anything over a 180 thread count. This will give you a very crisp and smart sheet. Percale feels beautiful, the only downside being it is quite difficult to iron and it needs ironing to look really good.

Sateen is woven using a different technique where the weft threads float across more of the warp threads. This creates a smoother and more lustrous sheet which is easier to iron and has a slight sheen.

Sleepy Silence

Your bedroom needs to be quiet. Heavy curtains in your bedroom – maybe heavier than you would naturally think – are a good way of blocking out external noise. Pay attention also to internal noise. Wooden floorboards upstairs can be beautiful to look at but troublesome when it comes to noise – something to think about if you have a large family and everyone goes to bed at different times. To avoid disruption, place soft rugs on the floor to absorb the sound.

Also make sure hinges are oiled and door handles open silently and smoothly. This is something you can make sure is right from the very beginning if you're starting out, but it's worth changing your handles if the sound of your partner opening the door every night when they come to bed disturbs you. The squeaky handle issue is also the reason that I have a love/hate relationship with ensuite bathrooms …

Being a very light sleeper with a career that involves extensive travel, I have trained myself to sleep with earplugs – a personal sound barrier that you can carry in your pocket. The most common types of earplug are foam or silicone. I prefer the little foam ones that you mould and then pop in your ear where they expand to block out sound. They may take a little getting used to but remember you can still hear – they just reduce the sound – so you will still be able to wake up to your alarm in the morning.

Bedroom Recipes

A Natural Nightcap

While you may not think of your bedroom as somewhere to eat, creating a nightly ritual is a really good habit to get into and can help you to get a great night's sleep.

Spiced Slumber Milk

This lovely warming cup of spiced milk is antioxidising, antibacterial and delicious. If you are using raw honey be careful not to add it when the mixture is too hot, as it will destroy its beneficial properties.

Serves 2

2 tablespoons chamomile flowers (or 2 chamomile teabags)
a thumbnail-size piece of fresh ginger, peeled and sliced
    (or ½ teaspoon ground ginger)
½ teaspoon vanilla extract
2 star anise
1 cinnamon stick (or ¼ teaspoon ground cinnamon)
3 cups coconut or almond milk (use coconut milk from a carton, not a tin)
1 tablespoon honey

Place all the ingredients into a pan and warm on the hob, but don't boil, allow to infuse for 10 minutes, keeping the heat very low. Remove and strain into a mug. Leave to cool for a minute, then stir in the honey.

Soothing and Calming Sleep Tisane

This is a powerfully seductive night time blend, conducive to a restful night's sleep. The lavender and chamomile are mild natural sedatives, the ginger, orange peel and peppermint will aid digestion and the calendula is said to lessen irritability. If you would prefer to use dried ingredients, double or triple the quantities and keep in an airtight jar, otherwise make this amount which is enough for two to three days, and keep the remainder in the fridge.

makes 4–6 cups

2 tablespoons fresh or dried rose petals
1 tablespoon fresh or dried lavender flowers
2 tablespoons fresh or dried peppermint leaves
2 tablespoons fresh or dried chamomile flowers
1 tablespoon orange rind
1 tablespoon fresh or dried calendula flowers
2 slices fresh ginger, peeled and lightly chopped
½ a cinnamon stick, lightly crushed

Put all the dry ingredients into a bowl and stir together using your hands. Add 2 to 3 tablespoons of tisane mixture to a cup or small teapot and pour over boiling water. Allow to infuse for 3 to 5 minutes. Strain and drink.

Honey Almond Milk

Almonds are high in magnesium and tryptophan, an amino acid that helps fight anxiety and induce calm. They naturally help the body to produce serotonin, a mood-balancing chemical which can encourage a good night's sleep.

Serves 2

120g whole almonds
400ml cold water
a pinch of pink Himalayan salt
a grating of whole nutmeg or a sprinkle of cinnamon
1 teaspoon honey

Soak your almonds overnight in cold water, making sure they are all submerged. The next morning drain, rinse and add fresh water, 1 part nuts to 3 parts water. Whiz in a high-powered blender until smooth.

Strain (if you like) through a fine sieve or muslin cloth – personally I don't mind the bits …

Warm your almond milk in a small saucepan but don't bring to the boil – it should be body temperature. Add the nutmeg or cinnamon and salt, pour into a glass with the honey, stir and drink.

Night night.

Breakfast in Bed

Is there anything nicer than breakfast in bed? It's a treat we should all indulge in more often – our very own version of room service. A lazy Sunday morning with pyjamas, the Sunday papers and a tray of delicious food … that is what enjoying life is all about. A tray made early on a Sunday morning, brought back up to bed to enjoy on your own with delicious food and coffee, is my version of bliss. It's an occasion that calls for some thought and consideration:

Get out a big tray. Lay a linen napkin. Arrange a flower in a small bud vase. Put butter in a small dish (go the extra mile). Use your best – or even better – your *favourite* teapot or the coffee plunger. Heat the milk in a lovely little jug

Now, what's on the menu? These are some of my favourite breakfasts, which you can mix and match as you please:

- Houston Street Granola
- Spiced Roast Plums
- Homemade Greek-style Yoghurt
- Olive Oil Folded Eggs
- Toasted Treacle Oat Bread
- Two Soft-boiled Eggs with Herbed Salt Sprinkle
- Buttermilk Scones with Almond and Brown Sugar Topping
- Freshly Made Bagels
- Very Berry Compote with Honey and Mint
- Dark Chocolate and Apricot Biscotti

Houston Street Granola

This is my favourite granola recipe and indeed what I eat most often for breakfast with plain (often homemade) Greek yoghurt. Sometimes I'll add fresh fruit, but more often than not just a handful of this with yoghurt sets me up for the day. I tried for years to recreate a bowl of granola that I had at a café on Houston Street in NYC. I couldn't put my finger on what I loved about this granola so much and it was only when, years later, I followed a recipe for sugar-free granola that it finally clicked, and with that first mouthful I was transported back to that café, eating that breakfast. The fact that it's sugar-free is a bonus, but for me it is simply the most delicious granola I know.

This is the basic recipe using almonds, apricots and cranberries, a favourite combination, but feel free to substitute with your own favourites – I change what I put in all the time, depending on my mood/what's in the cupboard. Recently I have started adding some cacao nibs which bring a beautiful earthy flavour, add after the first 10 minutes so they don't burn.

50g coconut oil
300g rolled oats
200g almonds
100g pumpkin seeds
50g linseeds
50g chia seeds
50g quinoa (uncooked)
1 teaspoon ground cinnamon
1 teaspoon fine sea salt
seeds from 1 vanilla pod or 2 teaspoons vanilla extract
125g cacao nibs
100g dried cranberries
100g dried apricots, chopped in half or in quarters

Preheat the oven to 180°C. Get two large roasting trays.

Melt the coconut oil by heating it in a small saucepan or the microwave. Put the oats, almonds, pumpkin seeds, linseeds, chia seeds and quinoa into one of the roasting trays and mix together with your hands. Sprinkle the cinnamon and salt on top and mix again once or twice.

Scrape the seeds out of the vanilla pod if using and add to the melted coconut oil (otherwise add the vanilla extract). Stir with a spoon then put the coconut oil mixture over the oat mixture. Mix well with your hands until all the dry ingredients are evenly coated.

Transfer half of the mixture into the second tray and spread out the contents of both trays before baking in the oven for 8 to 10 minutes. Take the trays out, stir and distribute the cacao nibs between both trays. Put them back in the oven and bake for a further 8 to 10 minutes, or until the oats are browned and the almonds toasted.

Remove from the oven and leave to cool completely before stirring through the cranberries and chopped apricots. Store in a large airtight container.

Spiced Roast Plums

I love a bowl of roasted stone fruit. If I'm having these for breakfast, then I like to roast them the day before and leave them in the fridge overnight to chill. This elevates my daily granola breakfast to a wonderful weekend treat. Equally a bowl of roasted stone fruit warm from the oven with a scoop of really good vanilla ice-cream is a delicious dessert.

Serves 2–4 depending on how hungry you are.

8–10 plums (or other stone fruit, such as peaches)
1 orange (juice of orange and zest of half)
1 tablespoon honey
2 star anise
2 small cinnamon sticks

Preheat your oven to 180°C.

Halve and pit your fruit, place in an ovenproof dish cut side up and squeeze over the orange juice and zest. Drizzle over the honey and add the spices.

Roast in the oven for 30 minutes to 1 hour – it will depend on the size of your fruit: you want it to be soft but not collapsing into a puree.

This recipe would work well with any stone fruit. Try apricots, peaches or nectarines. If the fruit is very sweet, you may not need to add the honey.

Homemade Greek-style Yoghurt

It really is so easy to make yoghurt at home: my parents constantly had large pots of it wrapped in blankets propped up against the back of the Stanley cooker in our kitchen. There are just a few steps but it's important to get each one right as you are working with a live culture here and you don't want to kill it. We all need to eat more live cultures and there is more and more research into the benefits of encouraging a healthy gut. The probiotics in yoghurt are the beneficial bacteria that help crowd out the bad guys and have a multitude of health benefits, there is also evidence that homemade yoghurt contains many more live cultures than shop-bought, so go ahead and make your own.

Makes 1 litre yoghurt

1 litre organic milk
2 tablespoons live yoghurt

Place your milk into a very clean pan over a medium heat. Warm the milk until it starts to steam but don't let it boil.

Remove from the heat and allow to cool to body temperature – check by placing a clean finger into the milk; it should feel neither hot nor cold.

Pour the milk into a large ceramic bowl, add the yoghurt and stir. You can now either place it in your hot press covered with a plate or cling film and wrapped in a small blanket or towel for 24 hours, or use the oven method.

Oven method:
While the milk is cooling, heat the oven to its lowest setting for 2 or 3 minutes at most until warm but not hot.

Pour the lukewarm milk with the added yoghurt into a casserole pot with a lid. Place the pot with the lid on into the oven and close the door. After 4 hours, check to make sure it's turning into yoghurt – it should appear slightly thickened. If your mixture is not thickening leave in the oven for another 4 hours or overnight.

When the yoghurt is done, place it in the fridge and strain for several hours to set and thicken.

When all of your milk has become yoghurt (through oven or hot press method) there is an extra step involved to transform it into creamier Greek-style yoghurt. Place a linen or cotton cloth into a fine colander or sieve and place over a bowl. Scoop the yoghurt in and leave it in the fridge to strain for 24 hours.

Olive Oil Folded Eggs

I was never really a big fan of scrambled eggs – a watery, lumpy pile on a plate – until I discovered this method for making them. It came to me by word of mouth but I believe it originates from Gordon Ramsay. The original version used butter but I decided to swap it for olive oil and I love the result. The trick to this method is temperature. You need to start with everything cold or at room temperature, put the cold eggs and oil into a cold pan and then warm and fold so that they make an emulsion resulting in the most divine eggs you will ever eat. You'll never go back!

2 free-range eggs per person
2 tablespoons good olive oil per every 2 eggs
a sprinkle of sea salt
1 teaspoon fresh thyme leaves per every 2 eggs

Crack the eggs into a bowl and add the olive oil. Whisk really well with a balloon whisk until you no longer see white and yellow but all is completely combined into one pale yellow frothy liquid.

Pour this into a cold non-stick pot. Cold is the key here. Add the salt. Now place your pot onto a low to medium heat and stir using a flat-bottomed wooden spoon or a spatula. Gently fold the eggs, constantly scraping the bottom until you see them start to stick. Add in the thyme leaves and keep folding gently, turning the cooked eggs over themselves until you have only the slightest bit of moisture left. You don't want to overcook them. Serve immediately with buttered, toasted oat bread.

Treacle Oat Bread

I spent a wonderful weekend early in 2016 in Ballintubbert House near Athy. Minnie, who owns it, has done an unbelievable job transforming it into a stylish and unique retreat that is available for weddings and other events. I was there for a wonderful weekend of yoga and cooking with my friend Lu Thornley who used to be co-owner of Lara-Lu Foods in George's Street Arcade. Lu now caters, mostly for weddings, and her food is divine, simple and full of flavour. There, Lu showed us a method of making bread that uses a yoghurt pot as the measure. I think this is genius as it means you can make this bread anywhere – you don't need a weighing scales. It's also highly adaptable: I've done lots of testing to come to this perfect combination of ingredients. I like the musky sweetness that the dark treacle adds, but if you'd rather leave it out, add 1 or 2 tablespoons of honey instead.

Makes 1 medium loaf

1 large 500g pot live full-fat yoghurt
1 free-range egg
3–4 tablespoons dark treacle
1 yoghurt pot of oats
1 yoghurt pot of wholewheat flour*
2 teaspoons baking soda
a good pinch of salt
a handful of each of the following or whatever combination appeals to you:
- linseeds
- pumpkin seeds
- chia seeds
- sunflower seeds

Preheat your oven to 180°C. Butter and line a 450g loaf tin.

Empty the yoghurt into a large bowl. Add the egg and treacle and mix well together.

Fill the empty yoghurt pot with oats and add to the bowl. Next add a pot of wholewheat flour. Spoon in your baking soda, salt and whatever seeds you want and stir well until combined (reserve some seeds to sprinkle). Empty the mixture into the tin, throw some seeds on top and bake for 50 minutes. Remove from the oven, turn out of the tin and place the loaf back in the oven for 10 minutes. You'll know it's done when the bottom sounds hollow when tapped. Allow to cool completely on a wire rack before slicing.

This bread can be sliced and frozen, so you have a lovely slice of bread for toasting at the ready whenever you fancy it.

* Sometimes I make this bread substituting the wholewheat flour for teff, which is now available in many supermarkets and most health food shops. I recently discovered this flour made from an Ethiopian grass and a fantastic source of fibre, protein and iron. It's got a distinct and robust flavour which works well in this recipe. Just substitute ¼ the amount that you use for the wholewheat flour, so ¼ of the yoghurt pot of teff (don't worry too much about getting it exact, the mixture will be quite runny). This would also make it a gluten-free bread.

Two Soft-boiled Eggs with Herbed Salt Sprinkle

The perfect egg is a very personal choice. Me, I like my eggs soft in the centre but the edges of the yolk should be just turning slightly solid. I know some people don't like runny eggs, if so boil the eggs for a minute longer. The herbed salt adds a wonderful flavour to a simple egg.

2 free range eggs

3 teaspoons sea salt

small sprig fresh rosemary

½ teaspoon pink peppercorns

½ teaspoon cumin seeds

First prepare the herbed salt. Finely chop the rosemary, add this with the pink peppercorn and cumin seeds to a pestle and mortar and give it a good few bashes to crush the seeds and break down the rosemary. Add the salt to this mixture and stir, then pour it into a little dish ready to sprinkle over your eggs. (You can make extra and store in a jar for next time).

Now cook your eggs. Bring a small pot of water to the boil, then reduce heat so you can maintain a rolling simmer.

Place your eggs on a large slotted spoon and dip into the boiling water and remove. Repeat once or twice – This will stop your shells from cracking as they acclimatise to the hot water. Boil your eggs for preferred amount of time:

- 5 minutes: firm white with soft centre
- 6 minutes: soft centre but slightly firming at the edges
- 7 minutes: centre is firm but not rock hard

Remove from the water with a slotted spoon.

Serve immediately with some toast soldiers and the herbed salt sprinkle on the side.

Buttermilk Scones with Almond and Brown Sugar Topping

I like my scones to be short and flaky, not spongy and springy (the texture you get when you use egg). The key to a good scone is in the method. You want to keep some of your butter in large pea-sized pieces, this creates the flaky texture. You also don't want to work the gluten in your flour too much, which will make your scones tough.

Makes 8 square scones

350g plain flour
1 teaspoon baking powder
½ teaspoon baking soda
40g light brown sugar
½ teaspoon sea salt
120g cold butter, cut into cubes
160ml buttermilk

For the topping:
additional buttermilk for brushing
40g almonds, chopped roughly
60g light brown sugar

Preheat the oven to 200°C. Combine all the dry ingredients in a large bowl and stir with a whisk to break down any lumps. Add the cold butter and rub together with your hands until you get a breadcrumb texture.

Add the buttermilk and stir gently with a fork to make a dough. Tip the dough out onto a lightly floured work surface and bring together into a mound, fold it over on itself and press down. Repeat this motion once more so it all comes together; don't overwork the dough.

Form the dough into a rectangle about 3cm thick, cut lengthways into two halves then cut each half into four square scones. Mix the brown sugar with the almonds. Brush the top of each scone with buttermilk and dip into the topping mixture. Place on a baking tin lined with parchment and refrigerate for 15 minutes.

Place in the oven and bake for 12–15 minutes until golden. Serve warm with butter and honey.

Freshly Baked Bagels

Having lived in New York for a total of 12 years, I felt it was my duty to include a recipe for these popular chewy mounds. There are two stages to cooking these but in fact there is not that much hands-on time. I promise you these are nothing like the flaccid rolls you buy in the supermarket – once you make them you may never buy one again. The dough is dense and stiff which is what you want from a bagel dough.

You need to begin the dough the night before you want to eat them.

In the recipe the water is given by weight not volume, this is common in bread making as it is easier to be precise. Simply pour your water into your weighing scales bowl and then add to the recipe.

Makes 8 bagels

2 teaspoons granulated sugar

1 sachet (7g) dried yeast

2 teaspoons salt

400g white bread flour

70g wholewheat flour

300g warm water

2 teaspoons honey (for boiling bagel
 water in the morning)

For the toppings:

Savoury (to cover four bagels)

¼ cup sesame seeds

¼ cup nigella seeds

¼ cup uncooked quinoa

2 tablespoons flaked sea salt

Sweet (to cover four bagels)

¼ cup uncooked quinoa

¼ cup sugar or sprinkles

2 tablespoons cinnamon

Plain but pretty (to cover four bagels)

cup of oats

¼ cup uncooked quinoa

Put all the dry ingredients into a large bowl. Stir to combine with a clean hand. Add the water and mix with your hand, kneading to make sure there are no bits of dry flour left – this should take 1 to 2 minutes. The dough should be dry and stiff. Bring to a round mass in the centre of the bowl. Cover with cling film or a plastic bag and leave somewhere to prove overnight.

In the morning turn out your dough (in my experience you do not need to flour the surface as this dough is very dry). Give the dough a light kneading for about 5 minutes, bringing it into a round. Let it rest, covered with a tea towel, for 10 minutes.

Divide your dough in half and then divide each half into quarters, leaving you with 8 small pieces of dough. Roll each piece into a ball. With a floured thumb, create a hole in the centre of each round measuring about 4cm in diameter. Cover the bagels with a clean tea towel and allow to rest for 30 minutes.

After 20 minutes, turn your oven on to preheat to 200°C.

Now, bring a large pan of water to the boil, add the honey and drop in as many bagels as will fit without them touching (in my largest pan I can fit

four). The bagels may sink to the bottom initially but should rise and float to the top within about 30 seconds. Boil for 1 to 2 minutes turning them over until they've just about doubled in size.

Scoop the bagels out with a slotted spoon and very quickly, while they are still damp, roll one side (the best-looking one) in the topping of your choice: rolling rather than sprinkling gives a much prettier and more abundant-looking finish. Place them on a baking tray lined with parchment. I usually like to make half savoury and half plain or sweet. Repeat the boiling and rolling method for the remaining four bagels, then bake them in the oven for 30 minutes until they are glossy and brown. Eat straight away.

You can freeze any leftovers – just remember to slice them in half beforehand for ease of serving.

Very Berry Compote with Honey and Mint

This is a lovely addition to your bagels – the honey and mint really complement the flavour of the fresh berries and it's really quick to prepare. This is also delicious in a bowl with some of your homemade yoghurt (see page 196).

1 punnet fresh raspberries (125g)
1 punnet fresh blackberries (125g)
5 sprigs of fresh mint
1 tablespoon honey

Chop or tear the mint leaves. Place them with all the other ingredients into a pan and warm gently on the hob, stirring and squishing the berries to release the juice. Leave to cool a bit then pour into a bowl. Serve dollops alongside the bagels.

Dark Chocolate and Apricot Biscotti

Sometimes first thing in the morning I just want something simple and sweet. This is a particular ritual I enjoy on a Sunday, when my youngest son and I are the first ones up and share some hours together before the rest of the brood arise. I prefer one of these to a Danish pastry, which can feel somewhat sickly first thing. The crack and crunch of a good biscotto dotted with dark chocolate and tangy apricots is the perfect partner to a strong morning coffee. And even more perfect if someone is bringing me this in bed!

Makes around 10–12 biscotti

1 free-range egg	½ teaspoon baking powder
75g caster sugar	75g apricots
125g plain flour	80g dark chocolate (at least 60% cocoa solids)

Preheat the oven to 180°C. Line a baking sheet with parchment paper.

Roughly chop the apricots and the chocolate and set aside. Whisk the egg and sugar together in a bowl with an electric whisk for 5 minutes, until you get a ribbon-like trail when you lift the whisk. Add in the flour and baking powder and fold together with a spoon. Stir through the apricots and chopped chocolate, mixing thoroughly.

Turn the dough out onto a lightly floured surface – it will be sticky but this is normal – and dust lightly with flour. Shape into a log about 25cm long and flatten to a 5cm thickness. Place this on your baking sheet and put in the oven for 25 minutes, turning it around halfway through the cooking time.

Remove from the oven and allow to cool for about 10 minutes. Then transfer carefully to a chopping board and slice the log into biscotti about 1cm thick each. Place these back onto the lined tray and bake for a further 10 minutes. Turn them over and bake for a further 5 minutes until crisp. Remove and cool on a wire rack.

Bathroom

The sacred ritual of bathing

has been embraced by

many cultures.

MANY OF US SEE THE BATHROOM as a functional room – a place in which to quickly shower, rub ourselves dry with a towel and maybe apply some make-up before getting on with the day. However, the bathroom is (or should be) a sacred space. The ritual of bathing has been celebrated and embraced by many cultures: Roman, Greek, Japanese and Turkish baths are all names that mean something and invoke a sense of cleansing and healing.

Public bathing began in Greece in the sixth century BC and the word 'spa' is derived from Sparta, an area in Greece. The idea of a hot-air bath – which was to become a sauna – originated here. In Rome bathing was a part of daily life – the public baths were not only a place to cleanse the body but also a place of great social importance where people gathered to gossip and discuss the daily news. Great bathhouses were built and people paid a small fee to attend and enjoy a ritual which involved first working up a sweat in a gymnasium, then swishing in and out of different baths of varying temperatures and finally being rubbed all over with olive oil by a slave. All very decadent indeed. A Turkish bath (hamam) involves an invigorating ritual of moving through rooms of warm, wet air of varying temperatures and bathing in warm and cold waters. In Japan, attending an onsen, a natural hot-water spring, is a tradition that is still a major part of Japanese culture and domestic tourism.

In Ireland bathing doesn't have the same illustrious or decadent heritage but that doesn't mean you can't start your own. To my absolute horror there seems to be a trend in new builds or refurbishments to omit the actual bath from the bathroom – a shower is deemed sufficient and convenient. Well, it *is* convenient – it will cleanse your body with a quick jet of water, but it cannot compare to the absolute delight and restorative quality of lounging in a hot bath.

For such a simple invention, a bath can deliver maximum impact on your wellbeing. A bath cleanses your *soul* and for me is one of life's great necessities. Bathing can be a time for meditation and reflection. Lying submerged in a warm bath is a feast for all the senses – your whole body enveloped with warm water, the scent of aromatic bath oils heavy in the air … a thirty-minute bath twice a week is a sensory ritual that should be prescribed for everyone.

A bath can moisturise and nourish your skin, supporting it and helping it to function to its maximum capability. Regular bathing can boost your metabolism, improve your digestion, eliminate toxins, clear your complexion and even help foster a restorative sleep pattern. To enhance the positive effects of bathing, salts, milk powders and essential oils can be added to the bath. Depending on what you use, these additions can help to detoxify your body, lower blood pressure and reduce fluid retention.

The temperature of the bath is important – immersing yourself in water of different temperatures has different effects.

- A hot bath (38–40°C) will help relax muscles, stimulate the lymph system, detoxify the body and clear the complexion.
- A cool bath (32–35°C) is recommended during pregnancy and also for rebalancing the nervous system and de-stressing.
- A cold bath (below 32°C) can relieve itchy skin, help mild depression and digestive issues and even ignite a waning libido!

Later on in the chapter I'll share some recipes for homemade beauty products which can really enhance the experience of bath-time luxury!

Getting the Look Right

The bathroom is generally the smallest room in the house, particularly the downstairs loo. I say this makes it a perfect opportunity to go a bit mad with the decor! Do something you might not have the confidence to do in your living room, push yourself right out of your comfort zone: create a bit of a surprise, go dark, go bright, go full-on clashing colour, go mad with wallpaper. Exploring your creativity in a small space is a great way to gain confidence in your decorating muscles.

I love a gallery wall in a small bathroom, where every inch of the wall is covered with pictures and photos for you to look at during every visit. Why not hang a favourite painting in your bathroom too? Then you get to enjoy it, in private, every day!

In an upstairs bathroom you may want to create more of a harmonious space where you can relax and de-stress. More than likely it will also be used to scrub muddy children or pets and service teenagers' many bathroom needs, so it needs to be functional too. Tiles are an obvious choice for bathroom flooring. I recommend going for a matt finish on floor tiles which makes them less slippery when wet. Terracotta tiles are a personal and timeless favourite for bathroom floors. Stone floors are beautiful, but are definitely an investment. If you can afford it and are laying a new floor, then *this* is the place to install underfloor heating.

Painted floorboards also work well and can really elevate the visual impact of your bathroom. You can buy high-gloss, water-repellent floor paint in any colour you can think of. Consider painting your floor in an unusual colour – I recently saw an all-white bathroom where the floor was painted a deep turquoise. The effect was sublime.

Tiles

Marble and natural stone will add texture and soul but you can get tiles with a translucent glaze and organic edges on the high street that will still feel luxurious, for less spend. Handmade tiles are an indulgence that will

add real warmth and a unique quality to a bathroom. Tiles with a slight colour variation in every batch have the most wonderful visual effect when used on a wall. Have a look in tile shops – often you can find something with real personality on the high street, you just need to search a bit.

Bathroom Plants

Plants are a welcome addition to any room, but they are particularly important in the bathroom. They not only add a necessary element of texture and colour to a room that is generally full of hard surfaces; they also add to the ambience and beauty and do a fantastic job of keeping your air fresh and clean. Plants filter out toxins and release fresh, clean oxygen into the air. I love to group together a lot of plants – this has significantly more visual impact and a greater effect on the air quality. If you don't have a windowsill, a small, high shelf is perfect for placing plants, or on top of a bathroom cabinet … anywhere really can work, even the basin ledge between the taps! A hanging basket is a good option if you are very short on space. The following plants are particularly good for filtering the air in your bathroom.

Peace Lily

Considered to be among the best air-filtering plants, they also thrive on the moist air created in a bathroom.

- Light: moderate and indirect sunlight
- Water: moderate, keep soil moist
- Toxic to cats and dogs if consumed

Snake Plant

Do not repot this unless necessary.

- Light: moderate
- Water: moderate
- Toxic if eaten

Golden Pothos

Very good for small spaces and works well in a hanging basket.

- Light: moderate to bright
- Water: low to moderate
- Toxic if eaten

Bamboo Palm

This is a good plant if your bathroom doesn't get much light.

- Light: moderate – will tolerate low light
- Water: moderate
- Toxic if eaten

Spider Plant

This is a really easy plant to propagate as it produces baby plants continually.

- Light: prefers bright light but will tolerate moderate shade
- Water: moderate – keep soil moist and do not leave in standing water
- Toxic if eaten

Aloe Vera

This is a great plant to have in your home: the sap can be used to soothe sunburn and minor cuts and burns. Make sure you use a wide rather than a deep planter.

- Light: bright light
- Water: low, leave to dry out between waterings
- Toxic if eaten

Touch and Texture

Surfaces in your bathroom need to be functional but warm and comforting too. Banish hard surfaces like steel and glass where possible and opt for natural and organic materials like wood (weathered wood even better), marble, bamboo, stone, cork. Do anything you can to avoid faux materials such as ceramic tiles that are made to look like wood or stone, you will lose the integrity of your space immediately!

It stands to reason that bathroom floors need to be warm underfoot as this is one of the main rooms in the home where we will be padding around barefoot – in all seasons. Cork is a wonderful option for a bathroom floor. If you are opting for stone or tiles, do consider underfloor heating – you won't regret it on those winter mornings. If you do not have it, then be sure to have some warm bath mats on the ground for when you step out of the bath or shower. Go for scale here – a minuscule bath mat will feel insignificant. I am a firm believer in placing conventional rugs instead of synthetic purpose-made bath mats down on your bathroom floor. Cotton dhurries, thick, flat woven cotton floor covers traditionally used in India, are perfect and can easily be thrown in the washing machine. Dhurries come in every colour conceivable and in many different patterns and are available from most home stores. For something plusher, take four bath mats and sew them together to make one large bathroom rug.

A heated towel rail is also something that will continue to give you pleasure long after you've forgotten the price tag. Wrapping yourself in a bathrobe warmed on your rail when you get out of the bath or shower will make you happy every time you do it. If space permits, try to include a chair in your bathroom – it can be a space on which to put clothes, bath-soak reading materials, or candles.

Keep your bathroom essentials such as toothbrushes and toothpaste in beautiful handmade ceramics. Throw your cotton buds, make-up pads, hair clips, etc. out of their generic plastic packaging and place these, too, in vessels with soul and personality.

The Importance of Towels

A towel is possibly the first thing that touches your body in the morning and last thing at night before you get into bed, so it makes sense to invest in quality. A beautiful plush cotton towel can be purchased these days at quite a reasonable price. There are different types of yarn, weaving and finishing processes that will affect the feel, absorbency and durability of your towel. I would only ever buy a towel that was 100 per cent cotton. All towels have a GSM (grams per square metre), which relates to the density of the fabric. Generally speaking, the heavier the GSM, the more luxurious the towel (the only downside is that they take longer to dry). A heavy, plush towel is nice in your master bathroom and you may select something lighter for the beach or gym where you will be carrying it around and want something more convenient. Here a lower GSM or flat-woven Turkish towel can be a great option, as it's light and dries quickly. For the most absorbent and luxurious towel select a low or zero twist: this refers to the amount of times the threads in the pile have been twisted – the lower the twist, the softer and more absorbent the towel. As when selecting your cotton sheets (see page 176), Egyptian cotton is the best quality because the longer fibres make for a better-quality and softer yarn. Also, a large towel, possibly a bath sheet, is a must in your master bathroom, so you can envelop your wet body completely. There's nothing worse than getting out of the shower and trying to dry yourself with a size-challenged towel!

To look after your towels don't use too much washing powder when washing them, generally speaking half of what you usually would use will suffice. Also do not use fabric softener on your towels as over time this will reduce the absorbency.

Sacred Ritual

Next time you take a bath why not make it into a ritual? Before you experience the soul-restoring feeling of immersion in warm, silky water, light a favourite candle or put some of your favourite essential oils in a diffuser. Scrub your dry body using one of the scrub recipes in this chapter, shower off then relax into a beautifully scented bath filled with salts. Close your eyes and relax in the moment.

Bathroom Recipes

Beautiful, Naturally

There's so much awareness now that what we put *in* our body affects our health and wellbeing, it's a natural progression to begin to think more about what we put *on* our body. Your skin is your largest organ, so I like to keep the products I apply to it as natural as possible, and what could be more natural than doing it yourself in your own kitchen? Making your own beauty products is a wonderful sensory experience. You can tailor-make everything to suit your own needs: your favourite scents and textures, just the right level of moisturising, detoxifying or calming. You prepare them in the kitchen just as you would with food recipes and often the end products are as enticing as something you would eat – it's a similar experience to preparing a beautiful cake, except they can leave you with a lovely glow.

Guidelines for Homemade Beauty Products

As these products do not use any preservatives or harsh chemicals, you must take care not to contaminate them and allow bacteria to grow, just as you would with your food. Here are some tips to looking after your homemade natural beauty products.

- Make sure the jars you are using are completely sterile. To sterilise jam jars, run them through your dishwasher then stand them on a baking tray and put in the oven for 20 minutes at 100°.
- Avoid direct sunlight or extreme heat. In other words, don't keep your jars on your windowsill.
- Don't let water get in to the mixture. Water will become a breeding ground for bad bacteria.
- Make sure your hands are immaculately clean and dry before dipping into any jars, or use a plastic spoon. The small ones they give away for testing ice-cream flavours are perfect.

Any recipe containing food products will generally have a short shelf life and you should only make it in small batches that will be used up quickly.

Coconut Salt Bath Soak

This wonderful bath soak will soothe and moisturise your skin. It has all the moisturising benefits of coconut and the detoxifying elements of Himalayan salt. Add your selected combination of essential oils to make it calming, comforting, de-stressing or a muscle relaxant.

Makes enough for 4–6 baths

Basic bath soak recipe:
200g creamed coconut (1 packet)
200g coconut oil
200g Himalayan salt

Select one essential oil combination:

Comforting (hot bath)	*De-stressing (cooler bath)*
10 drops bergamot oil	10 drops clary sage oil
5 drops sandalwood oil	6 drops lavender oil
5 drops frankincense oil	4 drops lemon oil
	(you can also add the zest from 1 lemon)
Muscle relaxant (hot bath)	
5 drops eucalyptus oil	2 drops black pepper oil
4 drops peppermint oil	4 drops ginger oil

Line a 450g loaf tin with cling film.

Unwrap the creamed coconut and place it in a bowl with the coconut oil. Melt together, either in a microwave or in a pan on a low heat. When the oil and creamed coconut are melted and combined and the mixture has cooled, add 100g of Himalayan salt and your selected essential oil combination.

Pour into the prepared loaf tin and sprinkle the top with the remaining 100g of salt, pressing down gently so it sticks to the top. Leave to set for a couple of hours. Store at room temperature. If you can spare the tin, I usually just keep it wrapped in the cling film in the tin. If not, remove from the tin and wrap completely in cling film or foil.

Slice a chunk off your 'loaf' and add to the bath as necessary (if the block gets very cold it may be difficult to slice – just warm slightly if this happens).

Soothing Oat and Honey Bath Bombs

These little bath bombs combine oats and honey with rose and soothing chamomile. Oats are incredibly moisturising for your skin, they contain saponin for cleansing and are rich in proteins and emollients, they can soothe rashes and helps with dry skin … you could call them a skin superfood! Honey also has moisturising and soothing properties and wheatgerm contains vitamins A, D and E and is nourishing and healing. The scent of the chamomile and rose is also calming. Add one or two to your bath as desired. I simply place these directly into my bath, but if you prefer not to have bits floating you can place your bomb into a little gauze bag. You may need to agitate the bomb a little to help it break down in the water. And keep out of the reach of children – they do look good enough to eat!

Makes 6–10 bombs, depending on mould size

160g oats
4 tablespoons honey
2 tablespoons wheatgerm oil
2 tablespoons dried rose petals
2 tablespoons dried chamomile flowers
8 drops petitgrain essential oil (or essential oil of your choice)

1 x silicone mould such as an ice cube tray (you could also simply roll these into balls but I don't think they look as pretty)

Pour your oats into a grinder (a coffee grinder is perfect) or food processor and blend to a fine powder. Pour into a bowl and add the rest of the ingredients.

Work everything together with your hands until it clumps together and when you squeeze it in your hand it holds its shape. Spoon into your chosen mould and press down firmly. Leave for a couple of hours to set.

Stored in an airtight jar, these will keep for up to six weeks.

Calming and Detoxifying Bath Salts

A very simple and quick combination for a soothing and de-stressing bath. Sprinkle a handful into running bath water as you are drawing your bath, then soak for at least 20 minutes to allow your body to benefit fully.

Enough for 1–2 baths

200g Epsom salts

50g Himalayan salt

a sprinkle of dried rose petals

6 drops of your favourite essential oil blended with a tablespoon of a
   carrier oil*

* 'Carrier' oils, such as almond or coconut oil, are used to dilute essential oils before applying them to the skin. Some essential oils applied 'neat' can cause skin irritation, stinging or redness in certain people.

Body Oils, Scrubs and Salves

Natural ingredients make fantastic body scrubs and all-over moisturising oils and salves. Once a week it's a good idea to give your body a good exfoliation to slough off all those dead cells – it makes your skin feel beautifully smooth and is good for your lymph system, which is basically your internal drainage system, and helps rid your body of toxins.

Body Oil

Rubbed into damp, warm skin after a bath or shower, body oils will leave your skin moisturised without feeling greasy. Combine the oils in the bottle and store at room temperature. Apply to damp skin after a bath or shower to get maximum moisturising benefits.

A Moisturising Floral Body Oil

40ml avocado oil
5 drops lavender essential oil
8 drops jasmine essential oil
5 drops chamomile essential oil
5 drops geranium essential oil
1 x dark glass bottle

All of these oils smell divine and have different properties. Combine the oils and add to the bath for extra luxury.

A Light and Invigorating Body Oil

40ml sweet almond oil
10 drops bergamot essential oil
5 drops lemon essential oil
5 drops clary sage essential oil
5 drops rosemary essential oil
1 x dark glass bottle

A Calming and Grounding Body Oil

40ml jojoba oil
10 drops rose essential oil
10 drops vetiver essential oil
8 drops frankincense essential oil
1 x dark glass bottle

Coffee and Brown Sugar Body Scrub

Coffee grounds and sugar are two very gentle exfoliants that are completely natural and will gently slough away dead skin cells which can clog your pores and make your skin appear dull and lacklustre. Stand in the shower and scrub this all over your body, starting at your feet and working your way up towards your heart. Work in a circular motion to remove any dead skin cells. Turn your shower on and rinse off thoroughly. This can be a little messy but it doesn't matter – you're in the shower and it all gets washed down the drain.

Makes 460g of scrub

200g ground coffee
200g brown sugar
60ml sweet almond or olive oil
3 drops frankincense oil
3 drops myrrh oil

1 x 500ml kilner jar or other container

Place the ground coffee and brown sugar into the kilner jar. Stir together to combine, pour over your oil and finally add drops of essential oils. This will keep for up to three months and probably longer. Store in the fridge when you are not using.

Magic Body Salve

I like to think of this not as a cream but a salve as it has such magical healing qualities on my skin. The texture is quite firm at room temperature but will liquefy upon contact with your body. I use it after a shower all over my body. I love the consistency of it. To wake up to baby-soft feet, slather it over your feet and put on a pair of old socks before getting into bed. It is also fabulous for your hands – especially if you are a gardener – or as a lip salve. Feel free to alter the combination of essential oils to your personal favourite.

Makes 160g of salve

60ml olive oil

60g coconut oil

20g beeswax pellets

20g cacao butter

3 drops eucalyptus oil

2 drops tea tree oil

5 drops frankincense oil

5 drops rosemary oil

2 drops geranium oil

1 x glass jar (a cleaned and sterilised jam jar works well)

Measure the oils and beeswax pellets into a small glass jar, such as a jam jar. Put the jar into a saucepan and slowly pour boiled water into the pan to come up to halfway up the jar. Be careful not to splash any water into the oil.

Stir the liquid until all the beeswax has melted (I keep a stack of wooden coffee stirrers for this purpose, as then you can discard after use – it is quite messy to remove the waxy residue from your spoons). You can also melt it in the microwave, heat for 1 minute and then at 30-second intervals until your beeswax is almost melted. Be careful when checking – the jar will be hot. Leave to cool for 15 minutes in the pan or microwave, until you can easily lift out the jar. Put the lid on and store in a cool, dark place. Apply as often as necessary until your skin is smooth and supple. Will keep for six weeks.

Face Masks and Oils

Natural face masks can deep-cleanse and restore that elusive glow to your complexion, while face oils moisturise deeply.

Glow Face Mask

This mask will leave your face feeling bright and tight. The oats and honey moisturise and the live yoghurt brightens. Apply liberally over your face, leave on for 10 minutes then rinse off with warm water. This will make a little more mixture than needed; it will keep in the fridge for two to three days.

Makes 2 face masks

2 tablespoons oats
2 tablespoons live yoghurt
1 tablespoon raw honey
1 tablespoon sweet almond oil

Pulse the oats in a blender or grinder to create a fine flour. Mix in a bowl with the remaining ingredients to make a fine paste. If the mixture is a little thick, add drops of warm water to get the desired consistency. Store any unused mixture in the fridge and use within three days.

● ● ● ● ●

Deep-cleansing Face Mask

This very simple mask using the combination of coconut oil and baking soda really gives your skin a deep clean. The baking soda normalises the PH balance of your skin and the honey helps to calm and moisturise. Apply all over the face, leave on for five minutes, then rinse off with warm water. Finish the treatment by applying some face oil.

Makes 1 face mask

2 teaspoons coconut oil
1 teaspoon baking soda
1 teaspoon raw honey

Leave the coconut oil in a warm place to soften a bit before you start making this mask. Scoop into a bowl, add the baking soda and honey and combine to make a paste. Apply to your face and leave for 5 minutes then rinse with warm water.

● ● ● ● ●

Moisturising Face Oil for Dry Skin

This face oil combines extremely moisturising oils with some essential oils that are beneficial to your skin. It is quite rich. Use sparingly, especially if you have oily skin. Start by applying a couple of drops to cleansed skin before bed twice a week, then you can build up to using it more often if you feel you need it. As with all products, pay attention to your skin and what it is telling you.

Makes approx. 60 ml

2 tablespoons apricot kernel oil
1 tablespoon wheatgerm oil
1 tablespoon rosehip seed oil

3 drops lavender oil
2 drops rose oil
2 drops geranium oil

1 x dark bottle

Combine all of the oils together in a ceramic bowl. Decant into the bottle. This will keep in a cool, dark place for six weeks.

Healing Oil for Oily or Combination Skin

Grapeseed and argan oils help reduce the production of sebum (oil) in your skin. Apart from smelling delicious, the combination of cypress and frankincense also helps oxygenate the skin, making this a great face oil for people whose skin tends to be oilier or prone to break outs. As with the oil above, apply a few drops at bedtime to cleansed skin.

Makes approx. 60 ml

2 tablespoons grapeseed oil
1 tablespoon rosehip oil
1 tablespoon argan oil
2 drops cypress oil
2 drops frankincense oil
1 drop tea tree oil
1 x dark bottle to store

Combine all of the oils in a ceramic bowl. Decant into the bottle, apply before bed.

Natural Cleaners and Air Fresheners

The air in your bathroom is possibly the most toxic in your entire home. This is the room, along with the kitchen, where we tend to use the most chemicals and toxins, as it's an important room to keep clean, hygienic and odour-free. For this reason, it's a great place to begin switching to natural products, as the fewer chemicals you introduce into your environment, the better.

· · · · ·

Taps

To keep taps clean and free from limescale simply rub with half a cut lemon or an old toothbrush dipped in white vinegar.

Bathroom Drain Freshener

Pour a slosh of white vinegar followed by a small handful of baking soda down your sink or bath drain. Leave for five minutes, then rinse with hot water.

Glass Cleaner

Vinegar is great for cleaning glass. To get a good shine, buff with old newspaper after spraying. Use 1 tablespoon of distilled white vinegar to ¼ litre of water, put in a spray bottle, spray onto glass and mirrors and buff with a soft cloth.

Air Freshener

Sometimes we need a little help keeping the air in the bathroom as fresh as we'd like! This air freshener will add a lovely, natural scent to your bathroom.

Air Freshener Spray

This spray is antibacterial and fresh with none of the toxic chemicals found in conventional fresheners. You'll need a 250ml spray bottle.

20 drops tea tree oil
20 drops rosemary oil
20 drops peppermint oil
10 drops lavender or lemon oil (depending on your preference)
6 tablespoons distilled water
2 tablespoons vodka

Combine all the essential oils in a ceramic bowl. Pour your water and vodka into the spray bottle and carefully add the essential oil mixture. Shake to combine.

Keep this in your bathroom cabinet and spray when you need a burst of freshness. Make sure to shake well before each use. It will last indefinitely but the oil scent may fade slightly as time goes by.

Outside

This is one place where

each and every one of your

senses is brought to life.

F YOU ARE LUCKY ENOUGH to have some space outside your home, whether it's a tiny city garden or a glorious swathe of green deep in the countryside, this is one place where each and every one of your senses is brought to life. Think about it – your eyes take in the living, growing plants, their variety and constantly changing beauty. You touch tiny buds, velvety leaves, smooth branches punctuated with knots. The fresh scent of greenery, loamy soil or perfumed flowers fills your nostrils. You hear leaves blowing, insects buzzing, birds … and you taste what might be growing there – a sharp, tangy bite into that bunch of chives growing by the back door …

Let me tell you about my journey to the Irish countryside and the garden I created there. It was 2002, I had two small sons, and I had returned to Ireland after a ten-year stint in New York. I had grown tired of carting a buggy up and down subway stairs, tired of sweltering summers and housebound days of winter when your face would freeze solid if left exposed to the elements. I had always known in my heart that I wanted to raise my children in Ireland. On 11 September, 2001 as I stood in my apartment in Brooklyn and watched the Twin Towers fall, I felt a sensation deep in my gut that I needed to return home. I needed to get my kids out of New York – I suppose it was my maternal instinct. The following July we arrived back in Ireland and moved in with my very gracious mother. We set about looking for a home, somewhere to raise our boys and put down roots. Maybe as a reaction to what was going on in the world or because I had been living in such a populated city for so long, I longed for a garden. No, I wanted more than that – I wanted land.

I don't mean acres – I wanted enough land to grow vegetables, have a garden, maybe chickens. Space. I wanted my children to be able to run barefoot and pick blackberries and build forts. We needed a house that had potential to build an outdoor studio for my work but nothing budget-busting, as funds were tight. The online property market was only just beginning – which seems incredible now – so it was there that I began to look at places. I needed somewhere close to Dublin – one or two hours' drive, and I didn't want a coastal town that relied on tourism. I found our Westmeath house and knew straight away that this was the place. I believe that buildings can hold on to energy that you can feel, and when I walked around this house I felt really happy energy. It was about 150 years old and had been the farm steward's house and part of a big estate. It had charm and character, it needed work but was structurally sound and the roof was good. It also had a large external garage that could easily be turned into a working studio for my textile business and three-quarters of an acre of land with fields on either side but neighbours not too far away to feel too isolated.

It took almost a year for the house to be ready for us to move in, but even before I had spent a night there I set about planting in the garden. I remember kneeling on the ground, with snow falling on my freezing hands, as I planted apple trees in the cold earth. There was nothing in the garden, just scutch grass, and as I discovered the following May, one enormous climbing rose with pale pink delicate double petals. I really didn't know much about gardening. My parents were both very keen gardeners and grew flowers and vegetables in every house we lived in. My mother passed on her knowledge and I pored over books, but mostly I learned from trial and error.

Things I Learned from Having a Garden

There is no such things as being green-fingered; there is just the doing. If you like plants and are prepared to care for them, then they will grow. If you stick them in unprepared ground and neglect them, then your chances of having a lovely garden with healthy plants are greatly diminished. It

really is that simple. Plants want to grow, so look after them, help and nurture them and they will!

1. Patience Is a Virtue

That foxglove seed you didn't want to plant because it wouldn't flower until its second year? After two years you'll be lamenting that if you *had* planted it you'd be looking at that stunning flower right now. That tree that was only 1 metre high and now gives you more apples than you know what to do with every year? Like children, a garden is a great marker of the passage of time. I learned my lesson many times to always read the label and consider the size of a plant when fully grown. It's hard to believe that little lupin plug you're popping in the ground will take up 30 x 60cm high of space, but if you overcrowd your plants you won't give them the best chance to thrive.

2. Do the Groundwork

Preparing in a garden means knowing your soil and your aspect. I never did soil test kits, although most garden books recommend you do. You can tell a lot by looking at your soil, picking it up and rubbing it through your hands. Is it sandy, gritty or sticky? Whatever the conclusion, you usually want to improve it by adding humus (organic matter) and nutrition (natural fertiliser or manure). Giving your plants the best possible soil to grow in is going to make gardening a much more enjoyable and successful pursuit. Also take into consideration how much sun your garden gets and plan your planting accordingly. Most plant labels will tell you how much sun a plant likes, or if it prefers shade.

3. Access All Areas

You will need to be able to get in to tend to your plants. So if your border is more than an arm's-reach wide, then provide stepping stones within it.

Otherwise you risk standing on precious shoots in the spring and damaging plants in the summer when they are in full swing.

4. Death Is Part of Life

Spring is hope – hope that this year everything will work out, hope that the garden of your dreams will become a reality. Inevitably though, things will not always go to plan. Some things will thrive and exceed your expectations; others will wither and wilt before your eyes. Just go with it. If something did very well in my garden I planted more of it, if something didn't then I left it out and moved on.

5. Repeat Yourself

Having lots of different plants is nice but don't go overboard. Repetition is key to success in a garden. As a rule of thumb I would say have at least three of everything you plant, depending on the size of your plot and the size of the plant. If you are planting bulbs, then more is better.

6. Don't Over-feed

Give your plants only the food they need. Generally, a feed in the spring is a good idea. But don't over-fertilise. Loading your roses with fertiliser hoping it will lead to abundant flowering can be the kiss of death for the plant. Greenflies feed on new growth, so if you encourage lots of new sappy growth by over-fertilising, you are encouraging greenflies, which lead to weakening, disfiguring blackspot. Some plants actually produce more flowers when they are growing in lean soil. Know your plants and what they want and feed them accordingly.

7. Little and Often

Like many things in life if you leave your garden untended for too long, it will become an even bigger problem. When it comes to weeding, little and often is the mantra to remember. Pay particular attention in spring, when weeds are just beginning to take hold – pulling them out now before they become established and spread will save you a lot of work in the summer. Watch out for pests too. A pest attack needs to be tackled as soon as it is detected.

8. You Can Grow Food

I know! But seriously, just do it, eating produce you've grown yourself is a joy we should all experience. No matter how big or small your space is, you can grow something. Cut and come again lettuce should be the first thing. Rocket is incredibly easy and the flavour is incredible. You can plant a blackcurrant bush in your flower border. If the idea of a vegetable patch seems overwhelming just stick a courgette plant in the ground or in a large tub. Also if you are thinking of planting a tree in your garden why not make it a fruit tree? As I write this Dublin is bursting with beautiful, spring blossom-covered trees and I can't help but wonder, what if they were all apple or plum trees? We could then not only enjoy the blossom in spring but also the fruit in autumn.

9. Design It

The most beautiful gardens will always think about colour. Some kind of very loose colour theme can really enhance the look of a garden. Maybe think of a family of colours as a theme, cool colours or hot and remember green is a colour too and foliage can play up or down whatever's beside it. Take into account when things flower – you could plan a garden that went from white in the spring to pink and reds in high summer.

10. Large Folks at the Back

Although it's true that you don't want to plant a shrub that is going to grow to 1½ metres high at the front of your border, planting some tall flowers or bulbs poking up through low-lying plants can be very effective. Imagine the purple heads of alliums poking up through a bed of acid green lady's mantle, or blue and white delphiniums surrounded by delicate nigella flowers. The long-stemmed *verbena bonariensis* with its delicate purple flowers also looks great poking through smaller plants. So as a general rule, yes put the larger plants at the back but also think about playing with this (especially with tall and skinny ones).

11. Gardening Is a Meditation

Our day-to-day activities have changed so much in the last hundred years. Phones, computers and televisions keep our brains constantly stimulated and in our drive to make life easier we have taken away many of the chores that gave us respite from our heads. I believe this is why meditation is having a resurgence. We need to meditate because we have taken away the repetitive jobs that gave us peace and respite from thinking, like washing-up, chopping wood or kneading dough for homemade bread. Well, gardening is one of these 'jobs'. Pottering about in the garden is not only good for the planet, it is good for your mind and your soul.

12. Let Go of the Results

A few weeds in my border don't bother me. Embrace the imperfection. Knowing when to step in and when to stand back comes from experience and experience comes from doing. Let things self-seed, let nature dictate, don't get caught up in a plan or an intention. Just start, and enjoy the ride.

The Sweet Scent of Home

Now that I spend most of my time in the city, it's the country air, the wet, sweet smell of grass and earth, the cleansing cloud of a gushing stream, the dark, earthy aroma of a mossy forest that I miss. In a place that is abundant in foliage, you can *smell* the green. It's not a sharp odour but a sweet, lingering fragrance that clears the head. In my Westmeath garden, there at the end of the path, between a large astrantia and a towering fennel and behind a prolific pink-fleshed apple tree, there's a spot. If I could bottle the perfume of that particular spot and dab it on every morning, my days would be happier indeed.

There are few things more rewarding than picking a scented bouquet from your own garden and placing it in your home or giving it to a friend. The smell of flowers has to be one of the greatest there is – a billion-euro perfume industry has been built on trying to capture the fragrance of petals, but you can grow your own beautiful scents for a lot less. I love to add herbs to my bunches – lemon balm, fennel fronds, sage, rosemary and chives: their spiced and sharp/sweet aroma adds an extra element of physical and aromatic beauty. A single fresh, scented flower beside your bed is a wonderful thing to wake up to in the morning. Below are some of my favourite scented flowers to cut and place around your home:

Sweet Pea

Watch out for unscented varieties, as not all sweet peas have a smell. Some of my preferred scented varieties are:
- 'Painted Lady' – two-toned pale and darker pink
- 'Mrs Collier' – pale cream
- 'Karen Louise' – lilac hued
- 'Janet Scott' – soft pink
- 'Albutt Blue' – white with bluish-purple edging.

Hyacinth

Next time somebody gives you a present of a potted hyacinth, plant the bulb outside after it has died down; subsequent flowers may be smaller but they will still smell beautiful.

Tuberose

This flower, native to Mexico, gives off its heady scent at night.

Scented Narcissus

This is incredibly easy to grow and one of the first spring flowers to bloom.

Stock

The beautiful scent of stock can be overwhelming if used on its own. Pair it with fresh herbs to cut through the sweetness.

Rose

I love a rose, and favour growing climbers and ramblers, as they are easy and far more abundant. When picking flowers for your house you don't want to have to be stingy. Don't assume all roses will be perfumed – some have no scent at all. Good scented varieties are:

- 'Margaret Merril' – white
- 'Madame Plantier' – many-petalled
- 'Heritage' – pale pink
- 'Mme Isaac Pereire' – mauvish-pink blooms with a powerful scent
- 'Alfred Carrière' – white climber
- 'New Dawn' – blush-pink climber
- 'America' – coral-pink climber
- 'Gloire de Dijon' – orange climber

Lily of the Valley

This is my mother's favourite flower and is most beautiful displayed solo.

Jasmine

Cut off a large trail of jasmine and place in a narrow vase. Or trim it down and include with roses and nigella. Grow the night-scented jasmine (*cestrum nocturnum*) outside a bedroom window – it's not much to look at, but heaven to smell as you drop off to sleep.

Honeysuckle

The heady scent of honeysuckle in your house is unbeatable. Tuck a long stem into any bunch of greenery or flowers.

Lilac

The stems of lilacs are woody and will need to be smashed with something to break them up – this helps them to last longer in a vase.

Lavender

Nobody can deny the enduring scent of lavender. Gather and dry to put into sachets for your clothes cupboards (see page 176).

Herbs

People don't always think about placing herbs in vases around the house, but all herbs have a wonderful aromatic scent. Place a bunch beside your bed or desk.

A bouquet made with many rose varieties, lupins, phlox, fennel, mint, lavender, astrantia and various grasses

Bringing the Beauty Indoors

It is one thing to revel in the look of your garden as you walk around it, drinking in the sight of your handiwork in the different seasons; it's another to bring the outside inside, so you can enhance the rooms of your home every day. I am often astounded by how many people grow flowers in their garden but never pick them to bring them inside.

Flowers and Greenery

Flowers are one of my passions. They bring life into a room. I'm not thinking of the elegant pruned showy arrangements you might see in a hotel or fancy department store, but the hand-gathered posies and billowy, blowsy things with tendrils reaching and trailing; soft, whispery fronds with delicate ephemeral petals that fall onto your mantelpiece.

Having my own garden was one of the things I missed most when I lived in New York. As I have said, there are few things in life that bring me more pleasure than wandering into the garden and gathering a bunch of flowers either for my own table or bedside or as a gift. If you have any patch of garden at all, I implore you to grow flowers for cutting. Shop-bought flowers are lovely and have their place and there are incredibly talented florists working in Ireland now. But a shop-bought, industrially produced flower will never compete with a home-grown specimen – the natural bend of a stem and unpredictable beauty, much like home-grown food, has a quality that cannot be reproduced on a mass scale.

If you have a spring-flowering fruit tree in your garden, cut some branches off and stick them in a vase. Evergreens and architectural leaves also look great brought inside, and can add a bit of individuality and drama to a shop-bought bunch of blooms. It's hard to go wrong but a vague colour theme like whites and pale pinks or blues and yellows helps your bouquets look pulled together. I like to add a lot of greenery to my arrangements and especially love adding herbs – mint, rosemary, thyme, even vegetables and salads that have gone to seed: rocket and coriander

White tulips.

A bunch of spring garden flowers mixed with fresh herbs.

Spring bluebells simply placed in a glass jar.

Garden flowers mixed with roadside 'weeds' like cow parsley.

that have bolted are a lovely addition to an arrangement. Generally, I add more greenery than you think you need – say three stems for every flower.

With the abundance of blooms that spring and summer bring, autumn and winter are my favourite times to use evergreens. The prolific conifer *leylandii*, which is the scourge of neighbours and gardeners everywhere, is particularly beautiful placed in a posie with roses or other autumn blooms. I love the idea that this tree, which is so unfashionable, gets a little moment to shine. I also love using euphorbia – the acid green and oranges of the leaves are so beautiful with red and plum tones from roses and dahlias. Take care when handling euphorbia, however, as its sap is a skin irritant. In the summer months the large-leaved gunnera makes a very dramatic centrepiece either as a single stem or multiple stems placed in a large vase. Any blossoming tree in the spring is obviously wonderful but don't be afraid to use bare twigs or branches in a posie in the wintertime – the effect can be beautiful.

It's tough to come up with a definitive list as truly I do love all flowers, but here is an attempt to give you some of my very favourites to grow for cutting. Most are not popular commercially in flower shops and so they will make your home-grown bouquets all the more unique:

Aquilegia

This flower is available in many colour and bloom types. Cut the stems long and let them hover above the rest of the bunch.

Astrantia

I grow blood-red and white versions, and also use the foliage.

Alchemilla Mollis

Also called lady's mantle, the acid green zing of these flowers can be seen in many an Irish country garden. They are very easy to grow and last well as a cut flower.

Cosmos

These delicate, long-stemmed blooms are easy to grow and last well as a cut flower.

Japanese Anemone

These flowers spread easily and even a single stem is beautiful in a vase. For maximum drama, keep the stems long.

Lupins

It's hard to find these in a flower shop so these will keep your arrangements unique. Lupins are beautiful in a vase. Be careful not to cut off new blooms that grow directly from the main stem. I also use the foliage often in bunches – it lasts for weeks in a vase.

Phlox

Pink and white varieties are available of this plant with tall stems and abundant small flowers. They are easy to grow and will self-seed if allowed.

Poppies

There are Icelandic, Californian and Oriental varieties of poppies. Seal the ends in boiling water after cutting and pick them right before the blossom bursts from its pod for maximum longevity.

Roses

All types and all colours of roses are a favourite and go with any other flower and foliage. A particularly spectacular bouquet includes many different varieties and hues of rose.

Tulips

Parrot, double and striped tulips always remind me of a Dutch master's painting. They bring great joy as they are one of the first flowers to bloom in spring (after daffodils).

Geraniums

This prolific plant can be invasive but if kept under control it's a very useful plant for flower arranging and can be used to fill a bouquet and allow the more showy blooms to shine. Cut the stems long and use the foliage in arrangements too.

Weeds and grasses

Don't be misguided by what you see in magazines or shops. *Any* plant can be a cut flower. I often add 'weeds' to my arrangements: dandelion leaves, grasses, cow parsley … also the greenery on plants grown for their flowers is often overlooked but is abundant and usually lasts well.

Nature's Song

You can introduce the sense of sound into your garden through your planting. Think of tall grasses swishing in the breeze. They also look impressive especially throughout autumn and winter when most plants have died back. Most grasses are easy to grow and tolerant of most soil conditions. See below for some of my favourite grasses.

Karl Foerster (Feather Reed Grass)

Like its common name suggests, this is a wonderful feathery upright grass and is one of the most popular garden grasses. Grows to 90cm high.

Miscanthus Sinensis (Chinese or Japanese Silver Grass)

This is a tall, silvery grass growing up to 2.5m high. It is a very popular plant throughout China and Japan. There are many different varieties but all have tall, slender stems with arching, feathery plumes that are particularly beautiful in late autumn.

Stipa Gigantea (Golden Oat Grass)

This striking tall grass can work really well at the back of a mixed border as well as integrated with other grasses. The tall golden spikes are dotted with oat-like spikes and are an airy and elegant addition to a garden. Typically grow to 2.5m tall.

Pampas Grass

This grass has had a bad reputation for being quite unfashionable but it can work really well when incorporated into a border or with other grasses. It is very easy to grow and looks very impressive when mixed with other plants. Just don't plant a single pampas in the middle of your lawn! There are around 25 varieties, ranging in height from 2–4m.

Briza Media (Quaker Grass)

This shorter native grass is better for the front of a border. It has beautiful

quaking seeds that make a wonderful noise when swaying in the breeze. It turns from a green in summer to golden in the autumn. Growing to 25–40cm high, it can be invasive if planted in your border.

As well as adding plants, the idea of sounds in your garden makes most of us think of one thing: beautiful birdsong. Poems, lullabies and songs have all been written about these magical tones. It is truly a marker of the beginning of spring when we start to hear the birds singing again. Suddenly one morning in January it is there, and you were not even aware that you missed it, but there it is in all its cacophonous glory.

It is mainly the male bird that sings, he bellows his heart out to attract a female. A strong and sustained song indicates a strong and healthy mating partner. It also warns off any potential competition – if a male approaches and hears a solid tune being whistled he will move on to avoid confrontation. Song is most abundant during the mating season (January to July) and most prolific in the mornings. This may be because many females lay their eggs and are most fertile in the morning, causing the males to sing as heartily as possible to attract them. Birds will sing and tweet at other times of the year but mostly to tell of a food source or warn of danger.

To attract more birds into your garden, place feeders where they can see them and also be on the lookout for any predators. Your lovely soft pussycat is potentially one of these so make sure the feeders are out of reach and not death traps! If you have the space, leave a corner of your garden to devote to a bird habitat – brambles and hawthorns attract birds and their thorny stems also act as shelter from predators. Leave out food that is high in fat and energy (especially in the winter). Examples of good bird food include sunflower seeds, peanuts and fat balls. It's easy to buy prepared feed in a garden centre but you can also make your own. It is also beneficial to leave them out some water in a bird bath (add a ping pong ball in winter to stop it freezing over). You don't need an expensive purpose-made bird bath, you could fashion something yourself from an old shallow tin bowl or even an upturned dustbin lid; don't use a ceramic bowl as if the water freezes it will crack.

It's a great idea to supply birds with a nesting box, but never put out a metal box or one with a metal lid as these can overheat in the summer and kill the baby birds inside. A box should be made completely of wood. There is also some thought that brightly coloured boxes attract predators. So plain or natural coloured boxes are better, just to be on the safe side.

Outside Recipes

The Taste of Summer

It is true that food just tastes better outside. A lowly supermarket sausage grilled over an open fire can take on legendary status. Sometimes we can balk at going on a picnic or eating outdoors but really you don't need very much and you can make something simple into an exciting adventure. A couple of loaves of bread with some cheese and fruit is all you need to make a lunch at the beach or in a country field.

Campfire Cooking

Cooking food over an open fire taps into something primal in us. In summer months when the nights are long we should all try to cook more outside. You don't need a fancy barbecue, although these are increasingly accessible and good value. In Westmeath we often cooked food outside on an open fire that was just a circle made of stones. The grill was an old fireguard and while we could have bought a fancy barbecue or built a snazzy outdoor fireplace, the simplicity of the stones on the ground was what appealed to me.

Campfire Flatbread

This simple flatbread recipe can be cooked in a conventional oven but takes on a new depth of flavour when baked over an open fire. Delicious wrapped around grilled meat, slathered with smoked tomatoes (see page 287), or just dipped in some olive oil.

Makes 10 flatbreads

500g plain flour (you can also use bread flour if you have it)
2 teaspoons dry yeast
1 teaspoon sugar
1 teaspoon sea salt
1 teaspoon ground coriander (optional)

350–400ml warm water

2 tablespoons olive oil

Place all your dry ingredients into a large bowl and mix with clean hands. Slowly pour in the warm water while using one hand in a circular motion to bring it together into one mass. Start by adding 350ml and then add more if needed – you don't want it to be sticky but you want no dry bits of flour left either.

Turn out the dough on to a lightly floured surface and knead for 5 minutes then place in an oiled bowl with a clean tea towel over it to rest for an hour.

Now turn out the dough and knead again, adding in the olive oil by drizzling it little by little into the centre of the dough and kneading in between. At first it may seem sticky but it will come together. Place back in the oiled bowl, cover and leave for another 2 hours.

Turn out your dough again and cut into 10 even pieces. Roll each piece into a tight ball and place on a large baking tray that you have lined with greaseproof paper. Cover and leave to rest somewhere warm for half an hour (leave a little longer if your house is cold).

Add fresh flour to your work surface and roll out each ball into a flat oval. Place over the hot grill for 2 to 3 minutes and then flip and bake the other side for a further minute. The time will vary greatly depending on the heat of your grill, but you want them to go over hot coals, not dying embers.

You could bake these in a conventional oven, preheated to 220°C. Just place on a heavy baking tray and cook for 2–3 minutes, 2 or 3 at a time. If your temperature is just right they may even puff up like pitta bread, leaving an airy pocket in the centre.

From marinated chicken thighs to simple supermarket sausages, everything tastes better when cooked over an open fire. The set-up does not have to be fancy – some stones on the ground and an old fireguard as a makeshift grill is all you need. Fruit and veg left to sizzle in the embers take on a smoky note that cannot be replicated.

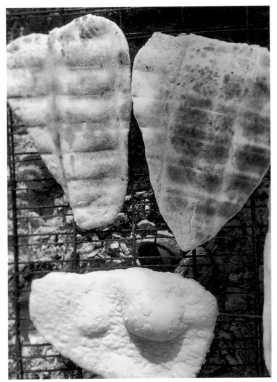

Charred flatbreads on the grill.

Charred Preserved Lemon

Charring the lemons before starting the preserving process adds a whole extra taste dimension to this Middle Eastern condiment staple. You only need the skin to impart flavour to a recipe – often a quarter or a half lemon skin will suffice.

3 unwaxed lemons
4 fresh bay leaves
1 teaspoon pink peppercorns
1 teaspoon sea salt
1 teaspoon coriander seeds
300–500ml olive oil (depending on container)

Cut the lemons in half and place cut-side down over the fire on the grill. Leave for 3 to 6 minutes then turn and grill on the other side. The time will greatly depend on your fire temperature, so you will need to judge yourself when they are done. You want a nice blackened and caramelised lemon (see photo).

Remove from the heat and place into a clean container like a sterilised kilner jar. Add the bay leaves, salt, peppercorns and coriander seeds then pour over enough olive oil to cover the lemons completely. Leave to infuse for at least 3 days.

Use these oil-preserved lemons much in the way you would use normal lemons or preserved lemons, in tagines or chopped and added to salads or couscous. An added bonus is that the oil is delicious in salad dressing or poured onto fish or chicken.

The lemons will keep in the fridge for 3 to 5 weeks.

Smoked Tomatoes

Smoky, roasted tomatoes, bursting out of their skins and fresh from the fire.

200g vine tomatoes
4 chive blossoms or chives (if flowers are not in season)
a sprinkle of sea salt

Place your tomatoes into a metal dish and sprinkle over the chive blossoms or chopped chives and salt. Remove the grill part from your fire or barbecue and place the tin sitting low into the embers. You want it placed like this so it catches the smoke and flavour from the fire.

Leave to cook until the tomatoes start to blister and the skins begin to burst, about 20 minutes depending on your heat. Carefully remove from the heat, pull off the stalk and stir into a thick sauce.

These are perfect with some flatbread, slathered onto some grilled meat, on a burger or on the side of practically anything! You can store any leftovers in a jar in the fridge for a few days, but I never have any of these left over!

Chermoula

Chermoula was originally created to marinate meats and fish in North African cooking. If you have time, pour this sauce over anything you will be barbecuing the night before you plan to cook it. My favourite, and I think the easiest, way to marinate something is to place the piece of meat, fish or chicken into a Ziploc sandwich bag, pour over the sauce and squeeze out the air before sealing. This way you are guaranteed all sides of the meat are covered in the marinade. Make sure you keep some of it aside after marinating your meat to drizzle on top after it has been grilled. It also works great over any vegetables, particularly courgettes and aubergines.

I like to make this in a large pestle and mortar, which gives it a lively texture, but make it in a blender or food processor if you prefer – just don't over-blend. The texture should be chunky, not smooth.

---

juice and zest of 1 lemon

½ teaspoon cumin seeds

½ teaspoon coriander seeds

2 large bunches of fresh coriander

3 cloves of garlic, peeled

½ teaspoon ground paprika

¼–½ teaspoon chilli flakes, depending on taste

a pinch of saffron

1 teaspoon sea salt

4 tablespoons olive oil

Put the lemon zest into the mortar, add the coriander and cumin seeds and pound with the pestle to break everything up and release their aromatic oils.

Tear up the fresh coriander and add along with the garlic, paprika, chilli, saffron and salt. Give this a good bashing to blend then add the lemon juice and olive oil and mix to a coarse paste.

Marinate your meat, fish or chicken overnight; if you are using with vegetables then just add before cooking. And remember to serve some on the side as a relish.

A Picnic Lunch

In the summer months, when the evenings are long and nature is at its most lush and fragrant, a picnic is a feast for all the senses. Forget about nasty plastic spoons and forks and instead treat your picnic as you would any other meal: gather those linen napkins, the real cutlery and your favourite blanket ... so they might make your basket a little heavier, but they will make the experience so much more enjoyable.

Aromatic Vegetable Pockets

On a picnic, you want food that is easy to eat and doesn't create a mess. These aromatic pockets are just the trick. Inside is spiced sweet potato and red peppers. The pastry is made with a hot crust that is sturdier than a short crust and is perfect for travelling. The nigella and fennel seeds add a beautiful fragrant flavour to the pastry.

Makes 8 pockets

For the aromatic hot crust pastry:
75g butter
100ml water
225g plain flour
a pinch of sea salt
1 free-range egg (beaten)
1 teaspoon nigella seeds (plus extra for sprinkling)
1 teaspoon fennel seeds (plus extra for sprinkling)
1 free-range egg (beaten, for sealing and brushing
   the top of the pockets)

For the spiced sweet potato filling:

1 medium onion	1 teaspoon cumin seeds
1 large or 2 small sweet potatoes	1 teaspoon mustard seeds

1 red pepper
2 tomatoes
1 tablespoon olive oil

½ teaspoon chilli flakes
200ml water

Place the butter and water into a saucepan over a medium heat and bring to the boil. Put the flour and salt into a large bowl, stir in the first beaten egg then add the hot butter mixture. Add the nigella and fennel seeds. Stir vigorously until everything comes together. Leave to cool for 15 minutes, then refrigerate for at least half an hour.

While the pastry is resting make the filling. Peel the onion and sweet potato; deseed the red pepper. Roughly chop the onion and tomatoes; chop the red pepper into very small pieces. Chop half your sweet potato into large chunks of about 1.5cm, then chop the other half very finely (or grate it). This will give your filling the mixed texture you want.

Heat the oil in a deep frying pan on a medium heat, add the onion and fry until softened. Add the sweet potato, pepper, cumin and mustard seeds and chilli flakes, stir for a minute then pour in the water. Add the tomatoes and cook at a simmer, stirring regularly, until the large pieces of sweet potato are cooked through and the mixture is dry, without any liquid left in the base of the pan. This should take around 10 minutes. Remove from the heat and set aside to cool.

When you are ready to make your pockets, remove the pastry from the fridge and cut into 8 equal portions. Roll each piece into a ball and then on a lightly floured worktop roll into a circle about 16cm in diameter. Preheat the oven to 180°C.

Brush the edges of a pastry circle with a little egg and spoon 2 tablespoons of filling on one half, fold over the other side and pinch the edges to create a seal. Brush the top of the pocket with beaten egg and sprinkle on some more nigella and fennel seeds if you wish.

When you've made all your pockets, lay them on a large tray lined with greaseproof paper.

Bake in the oven for 30 to 40 minutes until golden and fragrant.

Fruit Bars

These fruit bars can be made with a variety of fruit toppings including plums, rhubarb or pears. If you are using rhubarb I would double the sugar sprinkled on top. In this version I have used delicious fresh apricots and blueberries, both for their flavour and colour. The combination of coconut oil and butter in the base makes these crispy and just a little healthier. These are great for a picnic, or just anytime!

Makes 24 square bars

80g butter	a pinch of sea salt
80g coconut oil	500g fresh apricots (weight of whole fruit)
160g rolled oats	100g blueberries
160g plain flour	juice of a lemon
160g light brown sugar (1 tablespoon removed for fruit)	

Heat the oven to 200°C. Butter and line a 20 x 30cm tin.

Chop your apricots in half and remove the stone, sprinkle with a tablespoon of light brown sugar and squeeze over the lemon juice. Set aside.

Place the butter and coconut oil in a saucepan over a medium heat and gently melt. Place the oats, flour, sugar and salt into a bowl and pour over the melted butter and coconut oil. Stir to combine, then remove 8 tablespoons of the mixture to sprinkle on top of the fruit, set aside.

Press the remaining mixture into the tin until compact and even. Spread out your apricots cut side down on top then sprinkle the blueberries around them. Take the oat mixture you have set aside and crumble it on top.

Bake for 40 minutes until the fruit is bubbling and the top is golden brown. Remove and leave to cool before cutting into squares, then leave to cool completely in the tin. These will keep in an airtight container for 3 to 4 days.

Turmeric and Ginger Lemonade

This is a great way to add the health-giving turmeric and ginger into your daily life (see also page 91). It's a refreshing and healthy drink for a picnic or any time.

Makes just over 1 litre

200ml water
30g piece of fresh turmeric
60g piece of fresh ginger
6–8 tablespoons honey (start with 6 and add more at the end to taste)
juice of 3 lemons
1 litre cold or sparkling water

Peel and slice or grate the ginger and turmeric and put in a saucepan with the honey and water. Heat until boiling and allow to boil for 3 to 5 minutes or until the liquid is reduced by half. Remove from the heat and leave to infuse for 30 minutes.

Pass the liquid through a fine sieve into a jug. Add the lemon juice, stir and taste, adjusting the sweetness as necessary by adding a little more honey. Top up with plain or sparkling water and drink over ice, or decant to a bottle to bring on your picnic. Shake or stir gently before serving.

Cold Brew Coffee

A delicious, refreshing drink with a real kick to bring on your picnic. Making coffee this way allows you to really appreciate the complexity of flavour from a bean. Because you are not heating it at all you really get a different experience from regular or iced coffee, which can become bitter. The low temperature means your coffee is less acidic and therefore a more mellow flavour. A touch of cinnamon and sugar make this into something more like a chai. I like to make it with almond milk but you can use any milk you like. Make sure your coffee is very coarsely ground for this otherwise your cold brew will turn out cloudy. You will need a muslin cloth to strain the coffee through after it has steeped.

100g coarsely ground coffee beans
1 litre cold water
2 teaspoons brown sugar
a pinch of ground cinnamon
300ml almond milk/milk of choice (or to taste)

Put your coffee grounds into a large jug or bottle. Pour over the water and cover. Leave to steep on your worktop or in the fridge for 12 hours.

Now strain through a sieve lined with muslin into a jug or bottle. Add the sugar, cinnamon and almond milk and stir. Store in the fridge for up to 3 days, but if you would like to store it for longer (up to 2 weeks) just don't add the almond milk until serving.

Eating Flowers

I have been eating flowers all my life. I love a subtle floral undertone in a dish, but many people don't. So be judicious when adding flowers to food – you want a flavour, a hint. Here are some of my favourite edible flowers:

- Roses
- Calendula
- Nasturtiums
- Cornflowers
- Nigellas
- Pansies
- Lavender
- All flowers or seeds from herbs: thyme, rosemary, coriander, fennel, chives, basil and sage

Always make sure you are eating flowers that have not been sprayed with pesticides – don't eat flowers bought in a flower shop or gathered by the side of the road. The best rule of thumb is: if in doubt, don't eat it.

To harvest flowers for eating it is best to pick them at their peak, which is in the morning after any morning dew has dried. Leave on a paper towel in a cool place to allow tiny insects to crawl away. I do not wash my flowers as I know I have not sprayed them with anything and washing them can damage the delicate petals, but it's up to you. Flowers are best eaten the day they are picked but if you need to store them, put them in a plastic bag with a damp kitchen towel and place in the fridge.

Rose Petal and Lemon Biscuits

These biscuits are made using polenta, lemon and rose petals. The flavour of the rose is subtle and the polenta adds a wonderful crumbly texture. You can use dried or fresh rose petals.

Makes 16 biscuits

200g cold butter

zest of one lemon

100g sugar

a pinch of sea salt

200g flour

1–2 tablespoons sugar, for topping

100g polenta

petals from 4 roses (chopped) or 3 tablespoons dried rose petals

Put all the ingredients (except the sugar for topping) into a food processor and blend for a few minutes until a dough comes together. If you don't have a food processor simply rub the dry ingredients in to the butter, then add the rose petals and zest and bring it together to form a dough.

Tip out the dough onto cling film or baking parchment and bring together to form a cylinder. Squish with your hands through the cling film/parchment to get a nice tight, firm tube about 23 x 6cm. Transfer to the fridge for at least half an hour and up to 3 days.

Preheat your oven to 155°C. Line a baking tray with baking parchment. Remove from cling film or parchment and slice into 1 to 2cm-thick discs. Lift onto the baking tray and place in the oven. Remove from the oven after 30 minutes and sprinkle the top with the 1–2 tablespoons sugar. Turn the oven off and place the biscuits back in the oven for a further 10 minutes, then open the oven door and leave to cool fully *in the oven*. These last two steps are important – they make for a really light and crisp biscuit.

Honey, Garlic and Thyme Flower Tart

Cooking the garlic in the vinegar and honey before you add it really mellows the flavour of this tart, making it sweet and earthy. You can of course make this at any time of year, simply using the leaves of thyme instead of the flowers. This is a great tart for a picnic too and best eaten at room temperature.

Makes 1 x 23cm tart
8 slices

For the pastry:
160g plain flour
a pinch of sea salt
110g cold butter
1 tablespoon apple cider vinegar
60ml iced water
1 free-range egg, beaten (for brushing pastry surface)

For the garlic custard filling:
3 bulbs of garlic (cloves peeled)
1 tablespoon olive oil
1 tablespoon white wine vinegar
200ml water
1 tablespoon honey
1 tablespoon thyme leaves
180g grated cheddar cheese
4 free-range eggs
180ml crème fraîche
160ml double cream
a pinch of sea salt
freshly ground black pepper
20 thyme flowers
6 fennel fronds

First make the pastry. Place the flour and salt in a bowl and add the cold butter, cut into small pieces. Rub with your fingers until you get a fine breadcrumb-like mixture.

Add the vinegar to the ice-cold water and sprinkle onto the flour mixture. Work quickly and bring together into a dough, then turn out and press into a round. Wrap the dough in cling film and refrigerate for half an hour.

Heat the oven to 180°C. Remove the pastry from the fridge and roll out on a lightly floured surface to a 36cm round. Transfer to a 23cm tin and let the edges overhang. Place in the freezer for 10 minutes.

Remove from the freezer and line the pastry with parchment paper and baking weights or old butter beans. Bake for 25 to 30 minutes then remove from the oven, carefully take out the paper and beans or weights and brush the surface with a little beaten egg. Put back in the oven and bake for another 10 minutes. Leave to cool (but leave the oven on).

Now make the filling. Place your garlic cloves into a saucepan, cover with water and bring to the boil, cooking for 3 to 5 minutes. Remove from the pan and drain.

Dry the pan, pour in a little olive oil and fry the cooked garlic for 2 to 3 minutes until turning golden. Add the vinegar and water and cook over a medium heat for 10 minutes. Now add the honey and thyme leaves and cook until the liquid is reduced to a thick syrup just coating the garlic (about 5 minutes). Scatter the cheese over the base of the pastry case then distribute your garlic evenly over it.

In a bowl combine the eggs, crème fraîche and cream, season with salt and pepper and beat until thoroughly combined and no egg white or yolk are visible, just a creamy golden liquid.

Pour the custard over the garlic in the tart case and scatter the top with half of the thyme flowers and fennel fronds.

Bake in the oven for 35 to 40 minutes until the custard is just set but still has a little wobble in the middle. Decorate with the remaining thyme flowers and fennel fronds and serve warm or at room temperature.

A Floral Salad

This fresh-tasting salad scattered with fresh flowers looks as good as it tastes. The nuts and seeds add a nice crunch to the texture.

200g rocket
1 carrot
½ a cucumber
4 tablespoons sesame seeds (toasted)
2 tablespoons pistachios (chopped)
a handful of any combination of
    edible flowers or flower petals

For the dressing:
1 teaspoon orange blossom water
3 tablespoons olive oil
juice of ½ a lime
1 clove of garlic
1 teaspoon honey

Wash and grate the carrot, slice the cucumber and put into a salad bowl with the rocket. Peel and crush the garlic and combine with the rest of the dressing ingredients in a jar. Shake vigorously with the lid on until mixed.

Pour the dressing over the salad and toss, making sure everything is well coated. Sprinkle over the sesame seeds and pistachios, then scatter the edible flowers you've chosen on top.

Orange Blossom and Calendula Madeleines

Madeleines are always a delight but the addition of calendula and orange blossom water makes these ones extra special. You will need to start the process at least two hours before you want to cook them. You will also need a madeleine tin.

Makes 16–20 madeleines, depending on tin size

90g unsalted butter

2 free-range eggs

100g caster sugar

1 tablespoon honey

230g plain flour

1 teaspoon baking powder

zest of 1 lemon

1 teaspoon orange blossom water

petals from 2–3 calendula flowers

For the drizzle/garnish:

juice of 1 lemon

icing sugar

a few calendula petals

Melt the butter in a small saucepan and set aside. Place the eggs, sugar and honey into a bowl and whisk for 2 to 3 minutes until thick and creamy.

Add the flour and baking powder and fold in, then pour in the cooled butter, lemon zest, orange blossom water and calendula petals and stir until combined. Place the batter into the fridge for at least 2 hours, but preferably 8.

When the batter has had enough time in the fridge, preheat your oven to 200°C. Butter a madeleine tin and pour in your batter so that each mould is ¾ full. Bake in the oven for 5 to 7 minutes until golden. Remove and tip out of the tin to cool, then cool completely on a wire rack.

To make the drizzle, mix the lemon juice and icing sugar together until the sugar is dissolved, then drizzle over the madeleines. Garnish with some calendula petals scattered on top.

Index

Author acknowledgements

It takes a village …

Thank you to: Kerry McCall, Grace Terrinoni, Shivvy Roche, Emma Kelly, Kate Loudoun-Shand (Fred), Lu Thornley, Cliodhna Prendergast, Imen McDonnell, Susan-Jane White, Leigh, Tracy and Anne Tucker, Mel French, Vanessa Finlow, Catriona Archer. Craig Nethercott, Jason O'Brien, Fionn Davenport, Adrian O'Byrne, Farmer John, Colm O'leary, Pearse O'Byrne, Daniel Samya, Hugh Wallace, The entire Mayo Crew, Keith and Aisling and everyone at Fia.

Margaret Heffernan, Anne Heffernan, Sharon McMahon, Teresa Rafter, Stephanie Roche, Nicola Bowman, James Gould, Alex Brennan Kearns, Valerie Forde.

Verna James, Anna King, Lewis James, Murad James, Mark Geary, Gerry Spillane.

A very special thank you to Simon Watson for your incredible images, time and generosity, and to David Fernandez-Perez, Joanne Murphy.

To everyone at Hachette Ireland, particularly my editor Ciara Considine. Thanks also to copy-editor Susan McKeever.

Thank you to Rita Konig and Rachel Allen.

My three lights, Obi, Luan and Cy.

Picture acknowledgements

Simon Watson © endpapers, ii, vi (top middle; middle left; middle, bottom middle), viii, 19, 20, 23, 32, 36, 39, 50–51, 58, 72, 92, 112, 122, 124, 157, 159, 162, 174, 183, 184, 187, 188, 191, 193, 194, 197, 198, 201, 205, 207, 210, 213, 214, 219, 225, 231, 233, 234, 236, 239, 240, 243, 244, 250, 256, 260, 263 (left), 265, 278, 280, 290, 314.

Joanne Murphy © 9, 10, 17, 62, 71, 83, 88, 95, 102, 108, 118, 127, 134, 139, 143, 154, 169, 220, 288, 294, 297, 300, 303

Helen James' collection: v, vi, 5, 13, 14, 16, 21, 27, 28, 31, 40, 41, 52, 57, 68, 75, 76, 79, 81, 87, 93, 99, 101, 104, 107, 110, 120, 133, 148, 160, 166, 171, 177, 180, 209, 223, 255, 262, 263 (right), 268–9, 274–5, 276, 284–5, 287, 292, 299, 305, 306, 310

GAP Interiors: 26/Bureaux – Photographs: Greg Cox, 45/David Parameter- Lucy Moles, 47/ Bureaux – Photographs: Warren Heath, 66/Bureaux – Photographs: Greg Cox, 69/Costas Picadas, 117/ David Cleveland, 121/ Rachel Whiting, 128/Graham Atkins-Hughes, 214/ David Cleveland

iStock: 6/ Rike_, 177/ 49pauly